FROM QUESTIONS TO *ACTIONS*

USING QUESTIONNAIRE DATA FOR CONTINUOUS SCHOOL IMPROVEMENT

D1405772

BY

VICTORIA L. BERNHARDT, Ph.D.
Executive Director
Education for the Future Initiative
Professor
Department of Professional Studies in Education
College of Communication and Education
California State University, Chico, CA

AND

BRADLEY J. GEISE
Questionnaire Services Administrator
Education for the Future Initiative

EYE ON EDUCATION
6 Depot Way West
Larchmont, NY 10538
(914) 833-0551
(914) 833-0761 Fax
www.eyeoneducation.com

For information about permission to reproduce selections from this book, write:
EYE ON EDUCATION
Permission Dept.
6 Depot Way West
Larchmont, NY 10538

Library of Congress Cataloging–in–Publication Data

Bernhardt, Victoria L., 1952-
    From questions to actions: using questionnaire data for continuous school improvement / by Victoria L. Bernhardt and Bradley J. Geise.
        p.   cm.
    ISBN 978-1-59667-122-5
    1. Educational surveys. 2. Questionnaires—Design and construction.
    3. School improvement programs. I. Geise, Bradley J. II. Title.
    LB2823.B47 2009
    370.7'23—dc22
                    2009011199

10 9 8 7 6 5 4 3 2 1

Also Available from Eye On Education

DATA, DATA EVERYWHERE

Bringing All the Data Together for Continuous School Improvement

Victoria L. Bernhardt

TRANSLATING DATA INTO INFORMATION TO IMPROVE TEACHING AND LEARNING

Victoria L. Bernhardt

USING DATA TO IMPROVE STUDENT LEARNING IN SCHOOL DISTRICTS

(With CD-Rom)

Victoria L. Bernhardt

USING DATA TO IMPROVE STUDENT LEARNING IN HIGH SCHOOLS

(With CD-Rom)

Victoria L. Bernhardt

USING DATA TO IMPROVE STUDENT LEARNING IN MIDDLE SCHOOLS

(With CD-Rom)

Victoria L. Bernhardt

USING DATA TO IMPROVE STUDENT LEARNING IN ELEMENTARY SCHOOLS

(With CD-Rom)

Victoria L. Bernhardt

DATA ANALYSIS FOR CONTINUOUS SCHOOL IMPROVEMENT

Second Edition

Victoria L. Bernhardt

THE SCHOOL PORTFOLIO TOOLKIT:

A Planning, Implementation, and Evaluation Guide for

Continuous School Improvement (With CD-Rom)

Victoria L. Bernhardt

THE EXAMPLE SCHOOL PORTFOLIO

Victoria L. Bernhardt, et al.

THE SCHOOL PORTFOLIO:

A Comprehensive Framework for School Improvement, Second Edition

Victoria L. Bernhardt

ACKNOWLEDGEMENTS

Since 1991, *Education for the Future* has been creating and administering questionnaires for schools to help them with their continuous improvement efforts. I happen to think we have the best questionnaires, graphs, and services in the business. Our questionnaires are designed from research, revised, and updated on the basis of what teachers, students, and parents tell us are most important. A huge thank you to all who have helped design and improve our processes and products over the years. Another huge thank you to all those schools that have used and continue to use the questionnaire results to create better learning for their students.

In 1995, Brad Geise joined our staff. He helped us take our questionnaire services to another level, getting the questionnaires set-up online, automated, and available to any school that wants to use them. Brad, with the support of Sally Withuhn, has administered, analyzed, and graphed questionnaire results for literally thousands of schools around our country (as well as other countries).

The other members of our little *Education for the Future* staff, Patsy Schutz, Lynn Varicelli, and Augie Fash support the questionnaire work in many ways, including the writing of this book. I feel lucky every day to have such a dedicated and conscientious staff.

Several people reviewed and commented on the first draft of this book (which in and of itself was a real feat): Michael Derman, Pennsylvania; Robert Geise and Jeff Keller, California; Sowmya Kumar, Texas; Joy Rose, Ohio; Lisa McLaughlin, Oklahoma; and Kathy Miller, Jessie Rummins, and Laura Williams, Michigan. Robert Geise and Joy Rose read several drafts. Joy lovingly edited multiple drafts and made herself available to help with any task, any time. We are so fortunate to know and reap the benefits of Joy's generosity. She is our editor "extraordinaire."

Lynn Varicelli did a phenomenal job keeping the drafts and many, many edits of this book ordered and converted into a lovely layout. Lynn's work made it easy for the authors to keep going while working full time on other projects.

Brian and the staff at MC2 did a wonderful job on the cover.

A huge thanks to our publisher, affectionately known as *Cousin Bob,* Mr. Robert Sickles, and his staff. We are grateful for all you do to support the creation and marketing of all *Education for the Future* books. *Eye on Education* has to be the easiest publishing company in the world with which to work!

Thanks continue to go to my husband, Jim Richmond, for putting up with the ongoing writing process by letting me off the hook from indoor work and outdoor chores in the forest.

Sincerely,

Vickie Bernhardt
March 2009

Echoing Vickie's comments, many individuals have contributed to the content that follows. Perhaps most importantly, however, this book is a reflection of Vickie's willingness to travel to the ends of the earth (literally) to engage educators in improvement efforts. This book reflects the invaluable experience of doing the work in schools and districts, nationally and internationally, for many years and over many miles. Vickie leads *Education for the Future* by example, modeling a tireless work ethic that is fueled by the belief that systemic change is truly and immediately possible. I sincerely appreciate the opportunity to work hard with someone who dedicates every day to improving the lives of others.

Sally Withuhn, my partner in providing questionnaire services since 1995, deserves a special thanks for contributing to the development of a questionnaire process that has proven itself over time and has streamlined our work so that we are able to provide service to clients effectively and efficiently. She has continued to meet deadline after deadline for years. Many clients have Sally to thank for the effective presentation of their data.

I enjoyed working with my Dad, Robert Geise, on the text of this book. I will admit that he knows a thing or two about writing (not something that I would have offered so easily while I was in high school). I appreciated the opportunity and was proud to share my work with him during the writing and revision processes.

I owe a huge thank you to my wife Beth for contributing and supporting me in so many ways. She takes on my responsibilities at home when I am on the road, provides support at all times, and adds valuable insight from her experience as an elementary teacher. Many of our clients have seen photos of our three children, Benjamin, Ella, and Anna, who provide me with the ultimate inspiration and joy. My sincere hope is that this work will ultimately help inform Beth's work and improve the education provided for our children and for all children in schools everywhere.

Sincerely,
Brad Geise
March 2009

This acknowledgement section would not be complete without thanking you, the reader, and you, the school personnel working on continuous improvement, who believe in and use *Education for the Future* questionnaire products and processes. We are so honored to work with you.

We hope this book exceeds your expectations; if it does, it is because of the continuous improvement that has resulted from your insights, direction, assistance, and support all along our journey to improving teaching and learning for every teacher and student in every school—no matter its size or location.

ABOUT THE AUTHORS

VICTORIA L. BERNHARDT

Victoria L. Bernhardt, Ph.D., is Executive Director of the *Education for the Future Initiative,* a not-for-profit organization whose mission is to build the capacity of all learning organizations to gather, analyze, and use data to continuously improve learning for all students. She is also a Professor (currently on leave) in the Department of Professional Studies in Education, College of Communication and Education, at California State University, Chico. Dr. Bernhardt is the author of 14 books *(including this one)* eleven of which are still in print, all published by Eye on Education, Larchmont, New York. The books are listed on *Also Available* page iii.

Available about the time this book is published: Check the *Education for the Future* website (*http://eff.csuchico.edu*) for the link to our automated *SchoolPortfolio* tool.

Dr. Bernhardt is passionate about her mission of helping all educators continuously improve student learning in their classrooms, their schools, their districts, states, and provinces by gathering, analyzing, and using actual data—as opposed to using hunches and "gut-level" feelings. She has made numerous presentations at professional meetings and conducts workshops and institutes on the school portfolio, data analysis, process measurement, and school improvement at local, state, regional, national, and international levels.

Dr. Bernhardt can be reached at:

Victoria L. Bernhardt, Ph.D.
Executive Director
Education for the Future Initiative
400 West First Street, Chico, CA 95929-0230
Tel: 530-898-4482 — Fax: 530-898-4484
e-mail: vbernhardt@csuchico.edu
website: *http://eff.csuchico.edu*

BRADLEY J. GEISE

Bradley J. Geise, is the Questionnaire Services Administrator for *Education for the Future.* Brad joined the *Education for the Future* staff in April 1995 to support growing demands to provide evaluation support and questionnaire services for the School Portfolio process. He has conducted numerous workshops at local, state, and regional levels, in addition to co-presenting at national conferences with Dr. Bernhardt.

Brad directs the daily operations of the questionnaire services unit, placing emphasis on the integrity of data as well as providing the results that are most valuable and useful to schools. He works with clients from across the country, directing questionnaire services ranging from single schools to some of the largest districts.

In order to make questionnaire work more accessible to schools, Brad authored *School IQ: School Improvement Questionnaire Solutions*. Brad also authored *The Classroom Assessment Solution*, an application used to collect and analyze data for up to six assessments used in measuring early literacy achievement. This application is most frequently used to collect observational data at the classroom level, or to run batch analyses on existing data sets. Most recently, Brad has written an application that analyzes stranded/clustered assessment data.

Brad earned his B.A. in History from U.C. Berkeley. He then worked in the bay area as the Program Coordinator for the San Francisco Food Bank, managing a variety of community outreach programs and working on the first-ever study of hunger in San Francisco.

Brad can be reached at:

Bradley J. Geise
Questionnaire Services Administrator
Education for the Future Initiative
400 West First Street, Chico, CA 95929-0230
Tel: 530-898-4482 — Fax: 530-898-4484
e-mail: bgeise@csuchico.edu
website: *http://eff.csuchico.edu*

CONTENTS

PREFACE

In this age of educational accountability, school quality is often judged on the basis of student achievement test results only. It is very easy for schools and school districts to focus their data analysis efforts only on the measures "that count." Unfortunately, some schools are missing the fact that there are other data that can give them powerful information about how to ensure student growth at every level and in every subject area.

Qualitative data, especially questionnaire data based on well-constructed questions, can tell learning organizations so much about what needs to change to get different results. Questionnaire data can tell a school if its staff is ready for change and what staff members believe needs to change to get different results. Questionnaire data can tell teachers what students believe has to be in place in order for them to learn, and how to improve the learning environment. Questionnaire data can also tell a school and district what it would take to convince the community to vote positively for an educational bond or levy. This is powerful information since humans cannot act differently from what they believe.

With technology readily available and inexpensive (sometimes free), it is now possible to administer questionnaires to one hundred percent of any population you want to survey to discern their opinions and feelings.

Questionnaire data can help schools and school districts start their continuous improvement efforts from where they really are, saving the puzzlement about why improvement is not happening. Too often, well-intentioned learning organizations begin school improvement efforts from where they think they are, with respect to beliefs, collaboration, a vision, a solid plan, and leadership, as opposed to where they really are.

No matter the reason for administering a questionnaire, the steps in the process are similar—
- ▼ Start with a purpose—*what do you want to learn?*
- ▼ Adopt, adapt, or create an instrument complete with questions to get to what it is you want to know
- ▼ Decide from whom you need the information
- ▼ Determine a system to collect the data
- ▼ Administer the questionnaire
- ▼ Analyze and present the results
- ▼ Share the information

This book details the steps in questionnaire construction, administration, analysis, and presentation—from purpose to sharing the results. Each step in the questionnaire process is covered in a separate chapter.

After reading this book, you will be able to create, administer, analyze, and ultimately use questionnaires in your continuous school improvement efforts.

If you have questions, comments, or concerns about using questionnaire data, do not hesitate to contact either one of us. We really do want to support and encourage your work with questionnaire data as a part of your continuous school improvement efforts.

Sincerely,

Victoria L. Bernhardt, Ph.D.
Executive Director
Education for the Future Initiative
400 West First Street, Chico, CA 95929-0230
Tel: 530-898-4482 — Fax: 530-898-4484
e-mail: vbernhardt@csuchico.edu
website: *http://eff.csuchico.edu*

Bradley J. Geise
Questionnaire Services Administrator
Education for the Future Initiative
400 West First Street, Chico, CA 95929-0230
Tel: 530-898-4482 — Fax: 530-898-4484
e-mail: bgeise@csuchico.edu
website: *http://eff.csuchico.edu*

CHAPTER 1

UNDERSTANDING THE ROLE OF PERCEPTIONS DATA IN COMPREHENSIVE DATA ANALYSIS

This chapter describes how perceptions work with demographic, student learning, and school process data to help schools determine what needs to change in order to improve learning for all students.

In well over a thousand data analysis workshops, *Education for the Future* presenters have asked participants if they believe perceptions are important to know within the context of school improvement. We always get a resounding YES!! When asked why, workshop participants give responses similar to— "the public's perception determines whom we can get as students in our schools, and how much the public will help us"; "perceptions are people's reality"; and "we all have expectations and preconceived notions that determine how we act."

It is important to know what others perceive—particularly students, staffs, and parents who attend, teach in, and support our schools. All of us have perceptions of the way the world in which we live operates. We act upon these perceptions every day as if they are reality. Generally, we act in congruence with what we value, believe, and perceive.

All of us have perceptions of the way the world in which we live operates. We act upon these perceptions every day as if they are reality. Generally, we act in congruence with what we value, believe, and perceive.

The definitions of *perception* and its synonyms provide almost enough information to understand why it is important to know the perceptions of our students, teachers, administrators, parents, and—when appropriate—members of our communities.

The word *perception* leads us to such words as "observation" and "opinion," with definitions that include—

- a view, judgment, or appraisal formed in the mind about a particular matter
- a belief stronger than impression and less strong than positive knowledge
- a generally held view
- a formal expression of judgment or advice
- a judgment one holds as true

Synonyms include opinion, view, belief, conviction, persuasion, and sentiment.

- *Opinion* implies a conclusion thought out yet open to dispute.
- *View* suggests a subjective opinion.
- *Belief* implies often deliberate acceptance and intellectual assent.
- *Conviction* applies to a firmly and seriously held belief.
- *Persuasion* suggests a belief grounded on assurance (as by evidence) of its truth.
- *Sentiment* suggests a settled opinion reflective of one's feelings.

In organizations, if we want to know what is possible… we need to know the perceptions of the people who make up the organization.

Generally, we do not act differently from what we value, believe, or perceive. In organizations, if we want to know what is possible (i.e., if we want to know how others are perceiving what is possible), we need to know the perceptions of the people who make up the organization.

Gathering perceptions data can help us understand—

- *Values and beliefs*—what do teachers and staff believe will impact student learning and get all staff moving forward?

◆ *Shared vision*—are all teachers and staff on the same page, and do they know where they are going?

◆ *Organizational culture and climate*—how do school personnel work, and what needs to change to get everyone moving forward together?

◆ *Strategies that will help students learn*—what instructional and assessment strategies are being used, and are they working?

◆ *Teacher behavior*—what is actually being done—if teachers do not believe certain actions will improve student learning, they will not implement them.

◆ *What is important to students*—what do students believe has to be in place in order for them to learn?

PERCEPTIONS DATA IN THE CONTEXT OF DATA-DRIVEN DECISION MAKING AND CONTINUOUS IMPROVEMENT

Many schools in the United States believe they are being data driven when they analyze their annual summative student achievement test results—only. Schools know that disaggregating and analyzing student achievement results are extremely important and informative. However, using summative student achievement results alone can lead schools to implement short-term fixes. We see schools adding before-school programs, after-school programs, and remediation for the students not achieving. While these strategies could lead to immediate gains for some students, these "fixes" might imply that the strategies being used during the school day do not need to change, merely that we need to get the non-achieving students to "our" level of instruction. In effect, we are telling students who are having difficulty learning to sit quietly in their seats during class; we will attend to their learning needs after the achieving students have completed the day's assignments.

We want schools to provide strategies that will meet the needs of *all* students *all* of the time. To understand what needs to change to get different results, schools need to analyze their demographic and school process data in conjunction with their student achievement and perceptual results. In that way, each school will get a complete picture of the most quantifiable elements

To understand what needs to change to get different results, schools need to analyze their demographic and school process data in conjunction with their student achievement and perceptual results.

of the learning organization. Figure 1.1 shows these four categories of data and how they intersect to provide a complete picture of a learning organization. Understanding where a school is with respect to each of these categories and their intersections will inform schools where they are now and what they need to do to get different results. Analyses of these data can also tell schools if they are progressing to where they want to be.

MULTIPLE MEASURES OF DATA

Demographic data provide the context and show the structure of the school. Demographic data are powerful components of comprehensive data analysis; however, these data are often overlooked in data analysis. Demographics can begin to tell us about how students are treated and served (e.g., discipline, special education identification, gifted and Advanced Placement [AP] class enrollments, attendance, all by gender and ethnicity). Demographics can be corroborated with perceptions data (how students feel about how they are treated and served).

Perceptions data tell us what students (current and former) are thinking and feeling about the school and other important elements, such as what students believe has to be in place in order for them to learn. Additionally, perceptions can tell us what staffs are thinking and feeling about the learning environment; and, in the long run, what is possible with school improvement. For example, if staffs believe that the leadership does not support teachers in sharing and implementing a vision and that staffs do not work together to create a continuum of learning that makes sense for students, there is no plan that can be implemented that will create a continuum of learning for students until all staff members commit to the vision and determine how to work collaboratively with each other.

Student learning data tell schools how students perform at a given point in time on a specific measurement tool. If the formative and summative assessments measure what the school expects students to know and be able to do, when intersected with demographics and school process data, these data can tell teachers which strategies are working with which groups of students, and which processes are not working with which student groups. Listening to

Figure 1.1
MULTIPLE MEASURES OF DATA

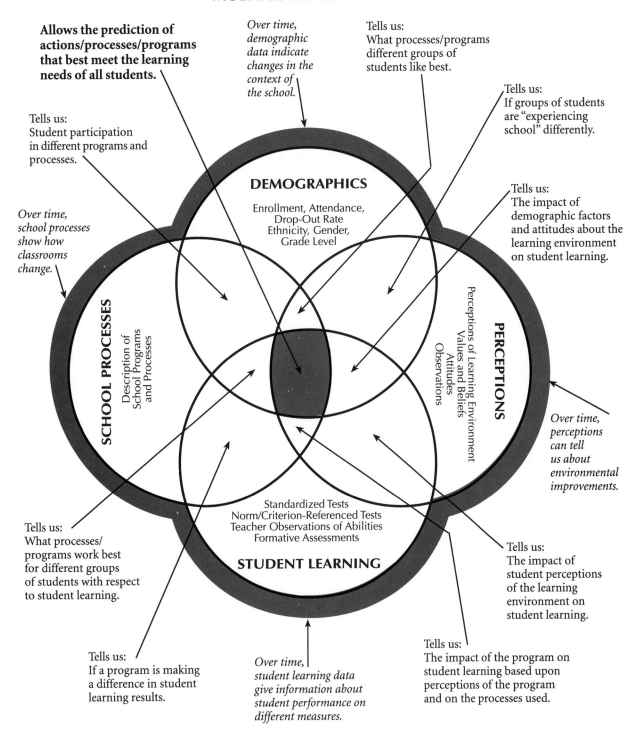

Allows the prediction of actions/processes/programs that best meet the learning needs of all students.

Over time, demographic data indicate changes in the context of the school.

Tells us: What processes/programs different groups of students like best.

Tells us: If groups of students are "experiencing school" differently.

Tells us: Student participation in different programs and processes.

Tells us: The impact of demographic factors and attitudes about the learning environment on student learning.

Over time, school processes show how classrooms change.

DEMOGRAPHICS

Enrollment, Attendance, Drop-Out Rate Ethnicity, Gender, Grade Level

SCHOOL PROCESSES

Description of School Programs and Processes

PERCEPTIONS

Perceptions of Learning Environment Values and Beliefs Attitudes Observations

Over time, perceptions can tell us about environmental improvements.

Standardized Tests Norm/Criterion-Referenced Tests Teacher Observations of Abilities Formative Assessments

STUDENT LEARNING

Tells us: What processes/ programs work best for different groups of students with respect to student learning.

Tells us: The impact of student perceptions of the learning environment on student learning.

Tells us: If a program is making a difference in student learning results.

Over time, student learning data give information about student performance on different measures.

Tells us: The impact of the program on student learning based upon perceptions of the program and on the processes used.

students' perceptions of the learning processes and the assessments can help teachers understand how to change their instructional strategies to get different results.

School process data tell us what programs are in place, and what and how instructional and assessment strategies are being implemented on behalf of students. Combined with demographic data, school process data can tell us about equality of access. Intersected, perceptions and school process data can inform us of what students are thinking and feeling about how they are being taught and how they prefer to learn, which can provide insight into how to change instructional strategies to meet students' learning needs. Intersected with student learning data, process data can tell us which instructional strategies or processes are working.

Together these four measures—*demographics, perceptions, student learning,* and *school processes*—help us see clearly whom we have as students, how they are being served, and the results the school is getting based on the way students are being served. If we want to understand how to improve services for all students, perceptions data just might provide the ticket to improvement.

If we want to understand how to improve services for all students, perceptions data just might provide the ticket to improvement.

CHANGING PERCEPTIONS

Is it possible to change perceptions? Absolutely. How do we get perceptions to change? The most effective way to change perceptions is through behavior changes. That means if some teachers do not believe in a strategy the majority of staff wants to take in all classrooms, one way to change their minds is to increase their understanding of the strategy and give them an opportunity to experience it. Awareness and experience can lead to basic shifts in opinions and beliefs, followed by shifts in attitudes. This is why staffs must include powerful professional learning designs (e.g., coaching, demonstration lessons, collaboration) in their continuous improvement plans. This is also why many schools have parent nights when there is a change in math, technology, or other curriculum. Giving parents an opportunity to understand and *experience* the approach helps them understand a different perspective, which could make them more supportive of the program.

Another way to change perceptions is through *cognitive dissonance*. Cognitive dissonance is the discomfort one feels when holding two or more thoughts, opinions, or ideas that are inconsistent. Cognitive dissonance creates perception changes when people experience a conflict between what they believe and what they, or trusted sources, experience.

In order to change the way business is done, schools must establish guiding principles that include the purpose and mission of the school. These principles grow out of the common values and beliefs about the factors that impact student learning for the individuals who make up the school community. Sometimes school communities adopt guiding principles that they *want* and *hope* to believe in, as opposed to those that they *do* believe in. The idea is that those who try out behaviors that are consistent with these principles will see a positive impact, leading to change in their internal thinking and belief in those principles. This is okay. *Changed attitudes represent change at the deepest level of an organization's culture.*

Too often, schools think of their guiding principles as being sacred and static. They might be sacred, but they should never be static. Even if a school keeps its guiding principles intact, their meanings evolve as people better understand, reflect, and talk about them as the principles are applied to guide decisions and actions. An example of behavior changes preceding perception changes follows.

> *Blossom Middle School teachers were given a questionnaire about their values and beliefs about technology—how they believed technology would increase student learning, and in what ways e-mail, the Internet, and videoconferencing used in instructional units would impact student learning. Students were given a questionnaire asking them similar questions and their impressions of the impact of technology on their learning. For two years, the results were almost the same; nothing was changing with respect to the implementation of technology and perceptions about technology in the classroom. In the meantime, teachers engaged in professional learning with demonstration and coaching components; administration placed typical staff meeting items on e-mail requiring teachers to begin implementing technology for personal use. With the coaching and demonstration lessons, teachers*

Cognitive dissonance creates perception changes when people experience a conflict between what they believe and what they, or trusted sources, experience.

Too often, schools think of their guiding principles as being sacred and static. They might be sacred, but they should never be static.

began implementing technology in their classrooms, leading to major behavior changes. During the following year, it became clear from the questionnaire results that the classrooms were different because teachers were using technology—first for their own benefit, and then with and for students. When their actions changed in the classroom with the use of technology, their ideas and attitudes changed about the impact technology could have on increasing student learning. It was also easy to see in the student questionnaire that student perceptions of the impact technology could have on their learning also changed—after the teachers' behaviors and attitudes changed.

Again, if we want perceptions to change—and we usually do as we implement new concepts and innovations, or as we try to get all teachers thinking the same way about implementing common strategies—we need to change behaviors. As the example above illustrates, to change student perceptions, teacher perceptions must change, which requires teacher behavior to change. A note about changing teacher behaviors: When we survey teachers about making desired changes in their classrooms, very close to 100% of the teachers who are not making changes related to implementing the vision or agreed upon strategies will say they are not doing so because they do not know what it would look like if they were implementing these strategies in their classrooms. Teachers must know what the instructional strategies will look like, sound like, and feel like when implemented. The implications for how professional learning is planned for, conducted, and supported are huge. Teachers must be involved in professional learning that is job embedded and includes practice and observation, such as peer coaching, demonstration lessons, collaborative observations, and ongoing support; they must be a part of the leadership structure, and understand that their job is to implement the vision. Sending one teacher to a conference for a day will not change that teacher's practice, or anyone else's in the school. Consequently, behaviors and, ultimately, perceptions will not change either.

If we want perceptions to change—and we usually do as we implement new strategies and innovations, or as we try to get all teachers thinking the same way about implementing common strategies— we need to change behaviors.

ANALYSIS AND USE OF PERCEPTIONS DATA CONTINUUM

Figure 1.2 is an *Analysis and Use of Perceptions Data* continuum that describes, on a one-to-five scale, how a school or school district might evolve from not using perceptions data for continuous improvement at a one level, to relying on these data to continuously improve practice. The continuum describes the theoretical flow of school improvement, evolving from a reactive (1) to a proactive (5) school.

Assessing on the *Analysis and Use of Perceptions Data* continuum helps staffs see where their systems are right now with respect to planning for perceptual data use, using perceptual data effectively, and the results they are getting attributed to the use of perceptual data. In addition to helping the entire staff see where the school is right now, the discussion begins to write the next steps the school needs to take to move forward on the continuum. Using this continuum over time will help staffs see that the school is making progress. If the school is making progress with perceptual data, chances are the school's student learning results are also improving.

The one-to-five point scale, moving from left to right, intersects with *Approach, Implementation,* and *Outcome,* top to bottom, to form a matrix that assists staffs in knowing where their schools are with respect to the systematic gathering, analysis, and use of perceptions data for continuous improvement. The continuum also helps staffs understand what they need to do to move to the right, or toward fives, on the continuum.

Approach refers to how a school is planning for, and talking about, the gathering, analysis, and use of perceptual data. *Implementation* reflects what it might look like if the school is taking that particular *Approach* to gathering, analyzing, and using perceptual data. *Outcome* presents the results a school should be realizing when it is *implementing* a particular *Approach.*

At Level 1, the school is not gathering perceptual data and, therefore, does not know what students, staffs, and parents are thinking or feeling about the school environment. The result is that many problems are never really identified and solved. Symptoms may be treated, but there is no true understanding of the underlying issues.

Figure 1.2
ANALYSIS AND USE OF PERCEPTIONS DATA CONTINUUM

	One	Two	Three	Four	Five
Approach	Data about perceptions of students, staffs, and parents are not gathered. There is no way to determine what needs to change at the school based on perceptions.	There is no systematic process for gathering perceptions of students, staffs, and parents. Questionnaires are administered only when required by an outside force, such as for accreditation or grants.	School collects data related to perceptions of current (and former) students, staffs, and parents. The information is used to drive the strategic quality plan for continuous improvement.	There is systemic reliance on all data as a basis for decision making and continuous improvement at the school level as well as the classroom level. Improvements are based on the study of all data, including perceptions of students, staffs, and parents; demographics; student learning; and school processes.	Information is gathered in all areas of student, staff, and parent interaction with the school. Teachers engage students and parents in gathering information on their perceptions of the learning environment to predict and prevent failures, and to predict and ensure successes. Accessible to all levels, data regarding perceptions are comprehensive in scope and an accurate reflection of school quality.
Implementation	No perceptual information is gathered with which to make improvements. Student and staff dissatisfaction with the learning environment is seen as an irritation, not a need for evaluation or improvement.	Some perceptual data are gathered and analyzed. Only a few individuals—students, staffs, and /or parents—are asked for feedback about areas of schooling.	Perceptual information from current (and former) students, staffs, and parents is analyzed and used in conjunction with future trends for planning. Identified areas for improvement are tracked over time.	Comprehensive data analyses are used to eliminate "contributing causes" of undesirable results and to improve the effectiveness of all school operations, especially instruction and the learning environment. Disaggregated perceptual results are graphed and utilized for improvement and to evaluate programs and processes.	Innovative teaching processes that meet the needs of students are implemented to the delight of students, staffs, and parents. Information is analyzed and used to prevent student failure. "Contributing causes" of undesirable results are known through analyses of all data. Problems are anticipated and prevented through the use of data.
Outcome	Only hypothetical information is available about the perceptions of current (and former) students, staffs, and parents. Problems are solved individually with short-term results.	Little perceptual data are available. The use of perceptual information for improvement is dependent upon individual teachers and their efforts, or requirements of an external agency.	Perceptual information from and about current (and former) students, staffs, and parents is shared with the school staff and used to plan for improvement. Information helps staff understand pressing issues and track results for improvement.	A comprehensive data analysis system is in place. Positive trends begin to appear in many classrooms and schoolwide. There is evidence that these results are in part caused by understanding and effectively using perceptual data and analyzing these data in conjunction with demographic, student learning, and school process data to eliminate "contributing causes" of undesirable results.	Students, staffs, and parents are delighted with the school's instructional processes and proud of their own capabilities to assess and improve the learning environment. Good-to-excellent achievement is the result for all students. No student falls through the cracks. Teachers use perceptual data to predict and prevent potential problems. The school uses perceptual data to evaluate the impact of programs and processes.

At Level 2, the school has begun to gather some perceptual data, although not in a systematic way. Some questionnaires are administered to a few individuals, usually to satisfy an outside requirement. The information is neither analyzed nor used for school improvement.

At Level 3, a commitment has been made to gather all types of data (i.e., demographic, perceptions, student learning, school processes) to drive school improvement. Questionnaires are given to current (and former) students, staffs, and parents to assess their perceptions about the effectiveness of all school operations. The questionnaires are analyzed, and results are shared to plan for continuous improvement.

At Level 4, all data (i.e., demographics, perceptions, student learning, and school processes) are used in a systemic way to drive decision-making and continuous improvement, in the school and in the classroom. Analyses of these data are used to identify and eliminate "contributing causes" of ineffective processes and undesirable results. Improved results can be seen thanks to the understanding and use of perceptual data, along with data regarding demographics, student learning, and school processes.

At Level 5, students, staffs, and parents are delighted with the instructional processes and the learning environment of the school. Demographic, perceptions, student learning, and school process data are systematically gathered, analyzed, and used to make decisions and to predict and prevent possible problems. Data analysis and its implications are shared with all constituents, and they are proud of their capabilities to assess and improve the learning environment for all students.

READER CHALLENGE

Using Figure 1.2, see if you can recognize where your school is currently with respect to the analysis and use of perceptions data. Also see if you can determine what your school needs to do to move up the continuum.

SUMMARY

Perceptions are one of four types of data that are important in continuous school and school district improvement. Perceptions can tell us what students, staffs, and parents are thinking and, ultimately, how they are acting. These data provide information for schools to understand what staffs need to do to improve learning for all students.

The chapters that follow provide the details about how to construct quality questionnaires and how to ensure that the administration, analysis, presentation, and use of the results are completed with the highest quality to ensure the reliability and usefulness of the results.

CHAPTER 2

MEASURING PERCEPTIONS WITH QUESTIONNAIRES: A PROCESS OVERVIEW

This chapter provides a general overview of the process of developing questionnaires to measure perceptions.

Common approaches to measuring perceptions in schools include the use of interviews, focus groups, and questionnaires.

Interviews with individuals allow for in-depth understandings of topics and content. Interviewing, which can be conducted in person or on the telephone, can be extremely valuable because interviews can provide the opportunity for follow-up questions not considered in the original design. Interviewing is, however, a labor-intensive approach to gathering perceptions data; and it is sometimes difficult to combine responses when the interviewing is completed.

Focus groups are small groups of representative people who are asked their opinions about specific topics. Focus groups of students are often used to understand what the larger group of students may be thinking. The downside of focus groups is that more people might want to contribute than those chosen to state their opinions.

Questionnaires are an excellent way to assess perceptions; they can be completed anonymously and re-administered to assess changes in perceptions over time. A questionnaire can collect information to describe, compare, and explain knowledge, attitudes, perceptions, and/or behavior. A questionnaire

Questionnaires are an excellent way to assess perceptions; they can be completed anonymously and re-administered to assess changes in perceptions over time.

typically consists of questions on printed paper or electronic pages. If the questionnaire is designed expertly, the administration and the analysis of the results are quick and easy.

OVERVIEW OF THE QUESTIONNAIRE PROCESS

No matter what the reason for administering a questionnaire, the steps in the process are pretty much the same—you need to start with a purpose; adopt, adapt, or create an instrument complete with questions to get to what it is you want to know. You also need the right people to take the questionnaire; a system to administer the questionnaire; a method for analyzing the results; and strategies for displaying, sharing, and using the results.

Figure 2.1 shows the major steps in the questionnaire process.

Determine the Purpose and Uses for the Questionnaire

To put together a valid (the "right" content), understandable questionnaire that is easy to complete and analyze, it is critical to think about and agree upon what you want to know or learn by administering the questionnaire, and how the results are going to be used.

> **DETERMINE PURPOSE:**
> **What do you want to learn? How do you want to use the results in conjunction with your school improvement plan?**

What do you really want to know? Why are you administering a questionnaire? To what end are you asking these questions? How do you plan to use the information? How will this information be used with your school improvement plan? Who is going to do the work? You might want to know perceptions of parents, students, teachers, and administrators with respect to a shared vision or what each constituency values and believes about school, education, teaching, and learning. These might be questions that you want to continue to ask over time to watch the responses change as new ideas and innovations are implemented. One might also want to know the degree to which standards are being implemented in classrooms. The use of this questionnaire would be to understand what would help teachers implement the standards.

Figure 2.1
QUESTIONNAIRE PROCESS

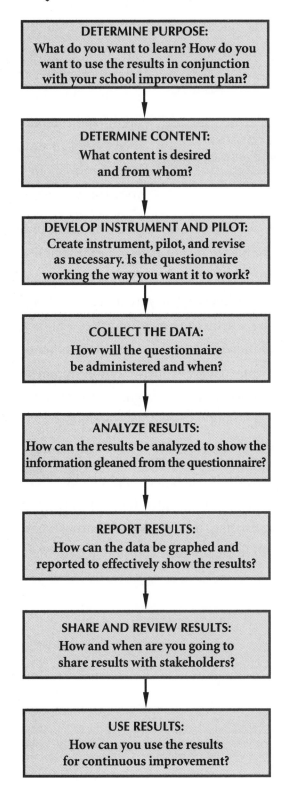

DETERMINE PURPOSE:

What do you want to learn? How do you want to use the results in conjunction with your school improvement plan?

DETERMINE CONTENT:

What content is desired and from whom?

DEVELOP INSTRUMENT AND PILOT:

Create instrument, pilot, and revise as necessary. Is the questionnaire working the way you want it to work?

COLLECT THE DATA:

How will the questionnaire be administered and when?

ANALYZE RESULTS:

How can the results be analyzed to show the information gleaned from the questionnaire?

REPORT RESULTS:

How can the data be graphed and reported to effectively show the results?

SHARE AND REVIEW RESULTS:

How and when are you going to share results with stakeholders?

USE RESULTS:

How can you use the results for continuous improvement?

Determine Content and From Whom You Will Gather the Information

Once the questionnaire committee has been established and has agreed upon the purpose of the questionnaire and how you will use the results, the next

> DETERMINE PURPOSE:
> What do you want to learn? How do you want to use the results in conjunction with your school improvement plan?

> DETERMINE CONTENT:
> What content is desired and from whom?

step is to brainstorm concepts that you want to measure, and to determine who will be able to give you the most information about those concepts. You might need to do a literature search to learn more about the specific concepts you want to study.

Identify whom you want to survey. As you think through the purpose for administering the questionnaire, determine the logical sources of information to answer the questions. When possible, you want to go directly to the source; i.e., if you want to know what parents are thinking, you need to survey parents. Consider whether the questionnaires will be given anonymously, if you will connect individual responses to data in other databases, or if you will ask for respondents' names or identification numbers. If you want honest, non-threatened responses, you might consider not asking for names or information that could identify the respondents. This depends on the purpose and uses of the questionnaire.

Check for existing tools. There just might be questionnaires already created that could be used, as is, or adapted for your purposes and uses. Always start with something existing, if it meets your purpose. Creating a questionnaire from scratch is difficult and time consuming to do well.

Develop the Instrument and Pilot

Creating the questionnaire can be a challenging task. Many people who want to design a questionnaire often stop when they begin formulating the questions because the job becomes too difficult. Writing the questions looks easier than it actually is. Writing good questions is labor intensive, but having good questions is the best way to get to the true perceptions of respondents.

> DETERMINE PURPOSE:
> What do you want to learn? How do you want to use the results in conjunction with your school improvement plan?

> DETERMINE CONTENT:
> What content is desired and from whom?

> **DEVELOP INSTRUMENT AND PILOT:**
> **Create instrument, pilot, and revise as necessary. Is the questionnaire working the way you want it to work?**

Pilot the questionnaire. No matter how many times you go over an individual question, no matter how many times you look at the questions collectively, you won't know how the questions will actually be interpreted until you administer them to a sample of respondents in your target group. It is imperative that you pilot the questionnaire and analyze the pilot data to ensure that you are asking questions that respondents understand.

Review pilot results. After the pilot responses come in, look over those responses very carefully. Consider each of the responses to the questions to see if each item was understandable. If you are including open-ended questions, look at the open-ended responses for clues to multiple choice responses you felt were not logical. Ask respondents, if they are available, to tell you why particular questions were hard to understand.

Revise, review again, and finalize. After you study the responses from the pilot group, revise the questionnaire to reflect what you have learned. Have several people review the questionnaire once it has been put into its final form to ensure there are no typographical errors and to ensure that the content flow is as you intend. You are then ready to finalize the questionnaire.

Chapter 3 provides the details for creating questionnaires.

Creating the questionnaire can be a challenging task. Writing the questions looks easier than it actually is.

It is imperative that you pilot the questionnaire and analyze the pilot data to ensure that you are asking questions that respondents understand.

Collect the Data

In data collection, we address two main issues—how will the questionnaire be administered and when. If you are able to use technology to collect questionnaire responses, it is recommended that you do so. Technology provides an effective and efficient approach to gathering data. When to administer questionnaires within schools and districts depends on the school calendar. Data collection is discussed in detail in Chapter 4.

If you are able to use technology to collect questionnaire responses, it is recommended that you do so. Technology provides an effective and efficient approach to gathering data.

Analyze Results

For questionnaires to be useful to the intended audience, the analysis must allow the audience to take action on the results. How the results are displayed affects the use and usefulness of the results. Chapter 5 describes and shows effective data analysis approaches for questionnaires, and Chapter 6 describes and shows effective presentation approaches for questionnaires.

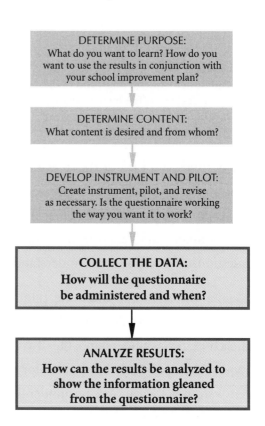

DETERMINE PURPOSE:
What do you want to learn? How do you want to use the results in conjunction with your school improvement plan?

DETERMINE CONTENT:
What content is desired and from whom?

DEVELOP INSTRUMENT AND PILOT:
Create instrument, pilot, and revise as necessary. Is the questionnaire working the way you want it to work?

COLLECT THE DATA:
How will the questionnaire be administered and when?

ANALYZE RESULTS:
How can the results be analyzed to show the information gleaned from the questionnaire?

Report Results

For questionnaire results to be used for improvement, it is necessary to present results effectively, in a timely fashion, and to provide avenues for the use of results. The primary goal for the entire process must be to move the analysis of perceptions data into reports that can be easily interpreted, and to get the results into the hands of the people that need them the most in time for them to use the results. Pages of complex disaggregated results should be reduced to individual and easy to read graphs. Our goal is the immediate and easy interpretation of results. More on this topic in Chapters 6 and 7.

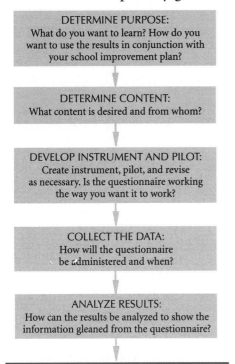

For questionnaire results to be used for improvement, it is necessary to present results effectively, in a timely fashion, and to provide avenues for the use of results.

Share and Review Results

For questionnaire results to be used, the findings must be shared with and analyzed by staff and stakeholders.

For the results to be used, the findings must be shared with and analyzed by staff and stakeholders. Different approaches to using the results with different stakeholders are described in Chapter 7.

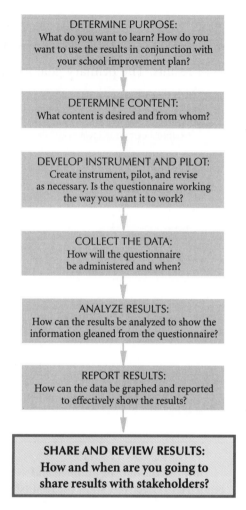

DETERMINE PURPOSE:
What do you want to learn? How do you want to use the results in conjunction with your school improvement plan?

DETERMINE CONTENT:
What content is desired and from whom?

DEVELOP INSTRUMENT AND PILOT:
Create instrument, pilot, and revise as necessary. Is the questionnaire working the way you want it to work?

COLLECT THE DATA:
How will the questionnaire be administered and when?

ANALYZE RESULTS:
How can the results be analyzed to show the information gleaned from the questionnaire?

REPORT RESULTS:
How can the data be graphed and reported to effectively show the results?

**SHARE AND REVIEW RESULTS:
How and when are you going to share results with stakeholders?**

Use the Results for Continuous Improvement

In order for questionnaires to be used for systemic improvement, the results must be integrated with the findings of demographic, student learning, and school processes data. These comprehensive data are analyzed and a continuous improvement plan is created. Chapter 8 delves into this concept.

From Development to Use

Chapter 9 details how the *Education for the Future* questionnaires were developed, administered, analyzed, presented, reported, and used.

As you go through the elements profiled in Figure 2.1, notice that the answer to one major step impacts previous and later elements. Elements should not be considered in isolation; how each one influences the others must be considered as the process is followed.

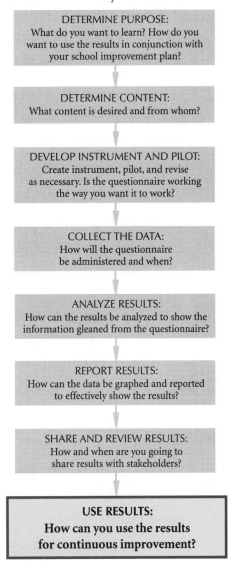

DETERMINE PURPOSE:
What do you want to learn? How do you want to use the results in conjunction with your school improvement plan?

DETERMINE CONTENT:
What content is desired and from whom?

DEVELOP INSTRUMENT AND PILOT:
Create instrument, pilot, and revise as necessary. Is the questionnaire working the way you want it to work?

COLLECT THE DATA:
How will the questionnaire be administered and when?

ANALYZE RESULTS:
How can the results be analyzed to show the information gleaned from the questionnaire?

REPORT RESULTS:
How can the data be graphed and reported to effectively show the results?

SHARE AND REVIEW RESULTS:
How and when are you going to share results with stakeholders?

USE RESULTS:
How can you use the results for continuous improvement?

Who is Going to Do the Work?

While administering a questionnaire may sound exciting—and it often is because of the information it can provide—it is easy for a committee to get carried into the project. There is nothing wrong with committees doing the work; however, very often the attention to detail required falls through the cracks if doing a questionnaire does not become the responsibility of one person. The person typically responsible for questionnaire oversight varies greatly from school to school. Many times the leader of the leadership team, an interested lead teacher, instructional coach, or data coach takes on the role to make sure the process is smooth and details appropriately attended to.

While the person responsible may not be expected to perform all the steps herself/himself—i.e., you want input from staff members to determine purpose, content, how, and when questionnaires will be administered—she/he must be sure that all the steps in the process are accomplished. Establishing a questionnaire calendar will keep the questionnaire process moving forward. The questionnaire coordinator must have the resources—time, money, and access to people—to do the job.

Establishing a questionnaire calendar will keep the questionnaire process moving forward.

Organizations such as *Education for the Future* can provide a variety of questionnaire services including content development, online hosting, scanning services, graphing and analyzing results, or consulting with a school or district to help it build its own capacity to facilitate questionnaire work.

Whether the questionnaire process is done in-house or through an outside organization, someone must coordinate the project at the school to ensure that the process is completed in a timely fashion and within the budget.

Whether the questionnaire process is done in-house or through an outside organization, someone must coordinate the project at the school to ensure that the process is completed in a timely fashion and within the budget.

READER CHALLENGE

If you have facilitated questionnaire work in the past, how does Figure 2.1 (page 15) compare to the process you used previously?

SUMMARY

The process of measuring perceptions through questionnaires is a multi-faceted task. Start by determining the purposes and uses of the questionnaire and who will oversee the work; ascertain what content and which type of participants will help achieve your purposes; determine whether the project should be done completely in-house, or if some of the elements can be done more effectively and efficiently by an outside source. After assessing that there are no other ways to get the information through an existing questionnaire or other data sources, develop, pilot, and administer your questionnaire. During the development phase, also consider how the results will be analyzed, reported, shared, and used.

CHAPTER 3

DEVELOPING EFFECTIVE QUESTIONNAIRES

This chapter discusses the elements of good questionnaire content and instrument development.

Good questionnaires have the following features:

- A strong purpose so participants will want to complete the questionnaire

- Short and to the point (both questions and questionnaires)

- Questions that everyone can understand in the same way

- Questions that proceed from general statements to more specific statements

- Response options that make sense for the questions

Whatever type of questionnaire you decide to use for data gathering, the questionnaire must be based upon the underlying assumption that the respondents will give truthful answers. To this end, you must ask questions that are—

- valid—ask the right questions

- reliable—will result in the same answers if given more than once

- understandable—respondents know what you are asking

- quick to complete—brain-compatible, designed well, and short

> *Good questionnaires have the following features: a strong purpose; short and to the point; questions that everyone can understand in the same way; questions that proceed from general statements to more specific statements; and, response options that make sense for the questions.*

- able to get the first response from the respondent—quality administration and setup

- justifiable—based on a solid foundation

Requiring respondents to read questions over and over in order to understand what is being asked, constantly reorienting themselves to the scale, or making it necessary for the respondents to gather information before they can complete the questionnaire, will increase the possibility of inaccurate responses, question responses left blank, or no response at all.

PLAN FOR THE QUESTIONNAIRE

To put together a valid, understandable questionnaire that is easy to complete and analyze, it is important to think through the elements of questionnaire construction and analysis before starting. Notice as you go through the elements profiled in Figure 2.1, that elements are interrelated; therefore, each element can impact either prior or later elements. Many issues must be taken into consideration, with a great deal of rethinking needed along the way. Figure 3.1 and the text that follows take an in-depth look at the first three boxes from Figure 2.1.

Figure 3.1
QUESTIONNAIRE AND INSTRUMENT DEVELOPMENT

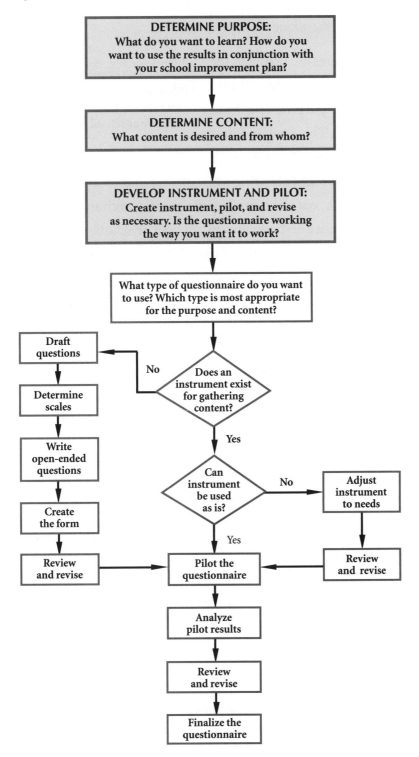

DETERMINE THE PURPOSE

What do you really want to learn? Why are you administering a questionnaire? To what end are you asking these questions?

There are no limits as to what can be measured with questionnaires in a school setting when one sets out to continuously improve all aspects of the system.

How questionnaires are used and the type of information sought will vary from purpose-to-purpose and from school-to-school. There are no limits as to what can be measured with

> **DETERMINE PURPOSE:**
> **What do you want to learn? How do you want to use the results in conjunction with your school improvement plan?**

questionnaires in a school setting when one sets out to continuously improve all aspects of the system. Some of the most common reasons to create, administer, and use questionnaires in a school or school district include, but are not limited to, those appearing below. The uses for the results would be to provide information to know how to improve.

COMMON REASONS TO ADMINISTER AND USE QUESTIONNAIRES IN SCHOOLS

Systemwide:
- Climate
- Culture
- Curriculum alignment
- Standards implementation
- Instructional coherence
- Staff collaboration
- Implementation of a vision
- Leadership effectiveness

Classrooms and Programs:
- Effectiveness
- Degree of implementation
- Participant preferences
- What is being learned
- What is being taught
- Satisfaction
- Ideas for improvement
- Assessment

It could be your school is administering questionnaires because the state requires them. Check the state guidelines and make sure you get the most out of each question to inform your school improvement efforts. Adding to the questionnaires to get specific information is better than administering two questionnaires.

Education for the Future questionnaires are offered as examples in the Appendix. The results of these questionnaires are used to understand the perceptions of students, staffs, and parents with respect to a shared vision, belonging, instructional coherence, to help staffs get to contributing causes of problems, and to get everyone's input on the climate of the school.

How Will the Results be Used?

To what end is this data collection activity directed? How will the information be used? How do you want to disseminate the findings? Do you need to present this information to a funding agency, to your school board, to parents and community, or to staffs for improving instructional practices?

The intended use of the information collected has a major impact on the questionnaire content. Results can be an effective way to convey climate and environment issues to those outside, as well as inside, the district for continuous improvement. Failing to report findings can result in a decrease in using data and also seriously impact your ability to get stakeholders to participate in future data collection efforts.

The intended use of information collected has a major impact on the questionnaire content.

DETERMINE CONTENT

What content is desired? What are you trying to assess? Can you get this information without doing a questionnaire?

Once everyone has agreed on the purpose of the questionnaire and how the results will be used, you will need to decide on concepts to measure, and who will be able to give you the most information about those concepts. You might need to do a literature search to learn more about the specific concepts you want to study, and you might need to interview others to determine how to best get the information you want.

> **DETERMINE PURPOSE:**
> What do you want to learn? How do you want to use the results in conjunction with your school improvement plan?
>
> **DETERMINE CONTENT:**
> **What content is desired and from whom?**

Check to see if it is possible to get the desired information without doing a questionnaire. Often, staffs inexperienced in questionnaire construction will want to ask questions that can be answered through other means. Consider an example question of parents: *Did you attend Back-to-School-Night?* If the purpose for asking the question is to find out how many parents came to Back-to-School-Night, there are other ways to know that information which might, in fact, produce more accurate data. Usually there is a guest book at Back-to-School-Night functions, or someone is put in charge of counting the number of attendees, so asking for this information on a questionnaire would not be good questionnaire protocol.

Avoid adding questions that can be answered by looking at data within on of the other multiple measures (demographics, student learning, or school process data).

Avoid adding questions that can be answered by looking at data within one of the other multiple measures (demographics, student learning, or school process data). In another parent example, consider: *This school is making progress in improving the achievement of all students.* The answer to this question can be uncovered most effectively by directly examining student learning results, unless, of course, you just want parent perceptions. Look to an appropriate source of information, and reserve questionnaires for important perception and climate questions that cannot be answered in other ways.

For example, the *Education for the Future* student questionnaires in the Appendix were suggested by teachers who wanted this questionnaire to be about what they wanted their students to be able to say by the time they had implemented their vision—that they feel safe at school, have freedom, have fun, and like school—theories from William Glasser's *The Quality School* (1990). Once you determine what you want to know, outline the key points and jot down ideas related to the key points.

Identify Whom You Want to Survey

As you think through the purpose, also consider whether the questionnaires will be given anonymously, if you will code them to link them with other databases, or if you will ask for respondents' names. *Education for the Future* questionnaires are given anonymously. We want honest indicators of how the whole school is performing. With respect to the purpose for administering the questionnaire and how it will be used, who or what are the logical sources of information? Who can answer these questions? When possible, you want to go directly to the source; i.e., if you want to know what parents are thinking, you need to ask parents.

Identify Subgroups for the Disaggregation of Data

As you decide to whom you want to administer the questionnaire, it is advisable to think of ways you will want to use the information in the end. If you want to disaggregate the data, think about the different subgroups you will want to pull out for the analyses and make sure you ask for this information on the questionnaire. For example, if you think there will be a difference in student responses by grade level and gender, you will want to ask students' grade level and gender on the questionnaire. This is information you cannot recapture after the questionnaire is administered.

You may want to disaggregate your questionnaire results by the same categories you will disaggregate your student achievement results—i.e., gender, ethnicity/race, indicators of poverty, English language proficiency, and students with learning disabilities, so you can make a comprehensive analysis, and understand more about your results. Typical disaggregations include:

Students

- ◆ Gender
- ◆ Ethnicity
- ◆ Grade
- ◆ Extracurricular participation (high school)
- ◆ Grade level when first enrolled in the school (high school)
- ◆ Plans after graduation (high school)
- ◆ School within schools identification

Staffs

- ◆ Gender (if there are appropriate numbers in each subgroup)
- ◆ Ethnicity (if there are appropriate numbers in each subgroup)
- ◆ Job Classification
- ◆ Grades and subjects taught
- ◆ Number of years of teaching
- ◆ Optional: Teaching Teams, Professional Learning Communities, etc.

Parents

- ◆ Number of children in this school
- ◆ Number of children in the household

If you want to disaggregate the data, think about the different subgroups you will want to pull out for the analyses and make sure you ask for this information on the questionnaire.

- Children's grades
- Native language
- Ethnic background
- Who responded (Mom, Dad, Grandparent, Guardian)
- Graduate of this school (high school)

DEVELOP INSTRUMENT AND PILOT

Decide on the Type of Questionnaire

In addition to the issues already considered, think about the best way to get the information. *Would it be through a questionnaire that the respondents actually get to look at, feel, think about, and respond to on their own time? Do you want their first thoughts or researched answers? Or will it be a questionnaire that will require respondents to use technology?*

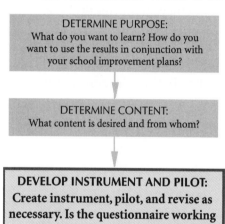

DETERMINE PURPOSE:
What do you want to learn? How do you want to use the results in conjunction with your school improvement plans?

DETERMINE CONTENT:
What content is desired and from whom?

DEVELOP INSTRUMENT AND PILOT:
Create instrument, pilot, and revise as necessary. Is the questionnaire working the way you want it to work?

Types of questionnaires include:
- Personal interviews
- Telephone interviews
- Mailed
- Paper
- Online

Figure 3.2 (pages 32-33) describes the pros and cons of using different types of questionnaires.

Answering the questions (on the previous pages) and determining which type or combination of types to use depend upon—
- your timeline
- the purpose for administering the questionnaire
- how many resources—time, money, people—you have available
- who is going to be completing the questionnaire, their availability, their technological skills, and the availability of technology

We highly recommend *not* using mailed questionnaires. Response rates are unacceptable, plus it is an expense that is no longer necessary. Most people in the targeted groups use e-mail and the Internet regularly and extensively and prefer using this approach. (More on data collection strategies will be discussed in Chapter 4.)

Does an Instrument Already Exist?

Before getting into questionnaire development, check to see if an instrument already exists for gathering the content you want. If an instrument exists, check to see if you can use it as is, or if you will be able to make adjustments that you might want. It is always better to go with something existing than to go through the effort of creating a questionnaire from scratch.

It is always better to go with something existing than to go through the effort of creating a questionnaire from scratch.

Draft the Questions

If there is no existing questionnaire to adapt, formulate questions that address issues based upon what you want to know. There are many different ways to ask questions. Figure 3.3 (pages 34-35) describes different types of questions, advantages and disadvantages for each type, and when it is appropriate to use a specific type of question. You can create forms that will allow you to use different types of questions; however, it is probably not wise to use more than two or three different types of questions in a form. The key is to make the questionnaire interesting, easy, and quick to complete.

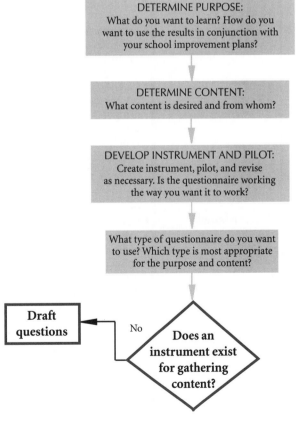

DETERMINE PURPOSE:
What do you want to learn? How do you want to use the results in conjunction with your school improvement plans?

DETERMINE CONTENT:
What content is desired and from whom?

DEVELOP INSTRUMENT AND PILOT:
Create instrument, pilot, and revise as necessary. Is the questionnaire working the way you want it to work?

What type of questionnaire do you want to use? Which type is most appropriate for the purpose and content?

Draft questions

No

Does an instrument exist for gathering content?

Figure 3.2
TYPES OF QUESTIONNAIRES PROS AND CONS

Types of Questionnaires	Advantages	Disadvantages	Appropriate When—
Interview *(Face-to-face)*	♦ Allows for in-depth person-to-person exchanges ♦ Might be the most appropriate way to get information from people with disabilities ♦ Can see evidence of change as well as hear about it	♦ Can be cost prohibitive; often need to pay interviewers and sometimes interviewees ♦ Requires extensive training and quality control to standardize ♦ Collating the responses is tedious, time consuming, and difficult ♦ Easy for the interviewers to change the questions	♦ You have a captive audience, such as students ♦ Physical changes are a result of the program ♦ You have a need to understand all aspects of change from the individuals ♦ Persons you seek to know about are physically or language impaired ♦ You have people trained to standardize questions ♦ The length of the questionnaire requires over an hour of a respondent's time
Telephone Interview *(Person-to-person)*	♦ Allows for the personal contact of face-to-face interviews, at a lower cost ♦ Can be done relatively cheaply ♦ Interviewers can enter responses into an electronic database as they interview ♦ Can hear individual perspective, while still using standardized questions ♦ People can usually be contacted quickly by phone	♦ Requires extensive training and quality control ♦ Might require interviewers to be able to speak different languages ♦ People do not like to be called for questionnaire responses ♦ Interviewers may change the questions slightly or greatly ♦ Interviewees might not answer all questions before they hang up the telephone	♦ People do not speak or read English ♦ You use the interview as a win-win, to connect closer to the community, to get people talking, and to add an element of public relations to your questions ♦ You have people trained to standardize questions ♦ You need fast results ♦ The technology is available ♦ Need less than 20 minutes of respondent's time (some say 10 minutes maximum)
Mailed	♦ Flexible ♦ Can gather a large number of responses ♦ Individuals can respond at their convenience ♦ Respondents can look up information if necessary ♦ Can include visuals (e.g., pictures)	♦ It is difficult to get an adequate return rate ♦ Must be able to write a compelling cover letter/ request to complete questionnaire ♦ Probably need to send two or three times ♦ Can be expensive ♦ Takes a long time to get to the point where you are ready to analyze results	♦ All perspective respondents are not present in one location at a particular time ♦ You need to ensure anonymity ♦ Respondents live out of the immediate area ♦ You have time ♦ You are not asking time-certain questions ♦ You can live with a small response rate

Figure 3.2 *(Continued)*
TYPES OF QUESTIONNAIRES PROS AND CONS

Types of Questionnaires	Advantages	Disadvantages	Appropriate When—
Paper	◆ Can give classes or groups oral instructions and guide them through the questionnaire ◆ Can be mailed ◆ Can easily include different types of questions and graphics to make it aesthetically appealing ◆ Responses can be scanned	◆ Requires knowledge about scanning, databases, and analysis of data to make analysis of responses easy ◆ Can be difficult and time-consuming to score if automation is not an option ◆ Cannot disaggregate easily if analyzing by hand ◆ Requires time to check the accuracy of the input procedure on every questionnaire response	◆ Documented comparisons of groups are desired ◆ Anonymity is desired ◆ Surveying large numbers of people ◆ Respondents are in many locations ◆ A large number of questions are required
Online	◆ Least expensive to administer and analyze of all methods ◆ It has an element of appeal ◆ Students and adults like to complete questionnaires using computers ◆ Can administer with computers networked to the Internet, in a lab, or on stand-alone computers ◆ Database can be automatically loaded as individuals submit responses ◆ Converts responses to numeric, electronic data immediately, removing a step that is present in other methods ◆ Open-ended responses get typed into the database by the respondent ◆ Easy to check for double submissions ◆ Fastest way to administer questionnaires	◆ May be difficult to get parents and community to complete computer questionnaires ◆ Not everyone has a computer at her/his disposal ◆ Still need to organize the administration as carefully as you would with any other data collection method ◆ It is difficult to complete in large schools with few computers—doable, just takes longer ◆ Need trained people to setup the questionnaire online	◆ School/organization has computer laboratories or a number of computers available to each classroom ◆ Ever possible, since the advantages far outweigh the disadvantages ◆ You need quick return of responses ◆ You can get your respondents to complete the questionnaire in person

Figure 3.3
QUESTION TYPE ADVANTAGES AND DISADVANTAGES

Types of Questions	Advantages	Disadvantages	Appropriate When—
Written *(Open-ended)* Example: *What do you like about this school?* (Write your response in the space provided below.)	◆ Spontaneity of the response ◆ Can understand what the respondent thinks ◆ Can get deep into the topic ◆ Can use to build multiple choice items ◆ Sometimes respondents provide quotable materials for program evaluation or advertisement ◆ Can ask all types of individuals, regardless of language differences	◆ Must pay for someone's time to transcribe and synthesize ◆ Takes time—on everyone's part ◆ Coding can be unreliable ◆ Cannot always read the response ◆ Some handicapped people might have difficulty responding ◆ Language translations are expensive ◆ Difficult to interpret ◆ Many people might have said the same thing with prompting ◆ Difficult to categorize when taking frequencies of types of responses	◆ Not sure about what respondents are thinking and feeling about a topic ◆ Want to gain insight into the respondents' thinking ◆ Are in the process of designing closed-ended questions ◆ Want to supplement or better understand closed-ended responses
Multiple Choice *(Nominal, Closed-ended)* Example: Suppose you are a school board member. What is the most important concept you think the school should focus on to ensure well-prepared students? (Circle the one response option below that best represents your position.) 1. Basic skills 2. Technology 3. Problem-solving skills 4. Lifelong learning 5. Collaborating with others	◆ Fast to complete ◆ Respondents do not need to write ◆ Relatively inexpensive ◆ Easy to administer ◆ Easy to score ◆ Can compare groups and disaggregate easily ◆ Responses can be scanned and interpreted easily	◆ Unless one has thought through how the items will be scored and has the capabilities of scoring items mechanically before sending out the questionnaires, it can be expensive to do, time-consuming, and easy to make mistakes ◆ Lose spontaneity ◆ Don't always know what you have as results ◆ Respondents are not always fond of these questions ◆ Some respondents may resent the questioner's pre-selected choices ◆ Multiple-choice questions are more difficult to write than open-ended ◆ Can make the wrong assumption in analyzing the results when response options are not the same as what respondents are thinking	◆ Want to make group comparisons ◆ Know some of the responses that the sample is considering, and want to know which option they are leaning toward ◆ Have large samples ◆ Want to give respondents finite response choices
Ranking *(Ordinal, Closed-ended)* Example: *Why did you choose to enroll your child in this school?* (Mark a 1 by the most important reason, 2 by the second most important reason, etc.) ____ It is our neighborhood school ____ Reputation as a quality school ____ Know someone else who attends ____ I went to this school ____ My child needs more challenge ____ My child needs more personal help	◆ Allows understanding of all reasons in priority order	◆ More than seven response options will confuse respondents ◆ May leave out important item response options ◆ Relatively hard to analyze—you will know the number of respondents who rated item one as 1, etc.	◆ Want to know all responses in an order ◆ Are clear on common response options ◆ Do not want people to add to list

Figure 3.3 *(Continued)*
QUESTION TYPE ADVANTAGES AND DISADVANTAGES

Types of Questions	Advantages	Disadvantages	Appropriate When—
Rating *(Interval, Closed-ended)* Example: (Circle the number that best reflects your response.) *I feel like I belong at this school.* Strongly Disagree — Disagree — Neutral — Agree — Strongly Agree 1 — 2 — 3 — 4 — 5	◆ Allows you to see the passion behind respondents' feelings, i.e., *Strongly Agree/Strongly Disagree* ◆ Easy to administer ◆ Easy to score ◆ Can compare group responses ◆ If an ordinal scale is created similar to the 5-point example, one can average the results ◆ There are many ways one can analyze the results ◆ Since there are usually only five options, frequencies of each response can be taken, along with the mode to determine most popular responses	◆ Do not know if every respondent is reading the question and response options in the same way ◆ Do not know what you have when *neutral* is circled—might be a bad question or the respondent doesn't care, or it might be a viable option ◆ Unless one has thought through how the items will be scored and has the capability of scoring items mechanically before sending out the questionnaires, it can be expensive to do, time-consuming, and easy to make mistakes ◆ Questions are more difficult to write than open-ended ◆ If charted together, questions must be written so the desired responses fall in the same direction (in other words—all written positively)	◆ Want respondents to rate or order choices, such as: *strongly disagree* to *strongly agree*, or show passion ◆ Want to make group comparisons ◆ Have large samples ◆ Want to understand where problems are in the organization
Yes – No *(Closed-ended)* Example: Yes No *I like this school* ☺ ☹	◆ Very young children can answer questions with these response options ◆ Very easy to score, analyze, and chart	◆ Not sure how meaningful the data are ◆ Responses do not give enough information	◆ Want all or nothing responses ◆ Have a sample that would have difficulty responding to more options
Nominal *(Categorical)* Example: (Please circle the best answer.) *I am–* Male Female	◆ Factual: no value judgment ◆ Useful for disaggregating other question responses ◆ Lets you know if sample is representative of the total population	◆ Some people will not respond to these types of questions ◆ Some people respond falsely to these questions ◆ With small groups, one might be able to identify the respondent on an anonymous questionnaire because of the demographic information given	◆ Want to disaggregate data by male/female, ethnicity, program ◆ Want to know the impact of a program on different types of individuals ◆ Want to know if respondents resemble the population

Be sure to ask purposeful questions—don't just ask questions for the sake of asking questions—and make sure many different people will interpret the questions the same way. Think about the impact of every question on your respondent. *Will it offend anyone?* Hints in developing the questions are summarized below. Helpful hints include—

- Simple is best.

- Phrase all questions positively. Movement up the scale indicates a more positive result; respondents will not be required to constantly reorient themselves to how the question relates to the scale, and results can be analyzed and graphed.

- Ask all questions in the same way (e.g., all positive so double negatives are not possible).

- Keep items and the questions short (definitely less than 20 words).

- Eliminate all jargon and bureaucratic wording.

- Spell out abbreviations and acronyms.

- Be sure that phrasing does not suggest a response.

- Use a logical sequence in asking questions (general to specific).

- Ask questions that everyone understands in the same way.

- Make sure that, if necessary, your questions will allow you to disaggregate responses in your analyses.

- List the question first and response options second (left-to-right is brain-compatible for most of the world).

- List response options from left (least positive) to right (most positive).

Avoid—

- Trying to assess a little bit of everything

- Conjunctions (i.e., and, or) in questions

- Adverbs such as "sometimes," "nearly," and "always" in the questions—let the response options discriminate responses

- Leading questions

- Jumping around content-wise

◆ Showing response options first and then the question—you are asking respondents to skip a part of the process and then come back to it—not efficient

◆ Asking the same question more than once

Determine Scales

Questionnaires are collections of items or questions intended to reveal levels of information not readily observable. Scales are used with items so responses can describe phenomena more specifically. Most questionnaires that utilize scales have a question or statement and then a series of response options. Those response options are types of scales. If you want to notice subtle differences in your analyses, you will want to use some sort of scale.

Questionnaires are collections of items intended to reveal levels of information not readily observable.

Types of Scales:

Many types of scales can be used with questionnaires. What type is used depends on the purpose of the questionnaire item and how the results will be used. General terms related to scales include nominal, ordinal, interval, and ratio.

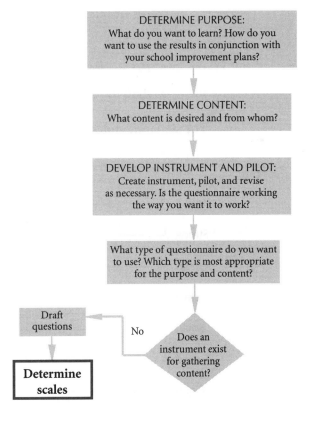

Nominal scales give numbers to categories, such as: 1=male, 2=female; *ordinal scales* provide information about direction and ranking, like from 0 (none of the time) to 10 (all of the time); *interval scales* create meaning between the intervals, such as a strongly disagree, disagree, neither agree nor disagree, agree, strongly agree; and *ratio scales* have equal intervals and an absolute zero point such as GPA, age, or number of years of teaching.

Specific uses of rating scales in education questionnaires include the following:

Continuous rating scales (ordinal) most often run from zero to one hundred. These are the types of scales used when you want respondents to place a mark on a line to indicate their response. An example is shown below.

ORDINAL EXAMPLE

What percentage of the time would you say you teach to the state standards in your classroom?

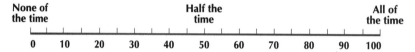

With *semantic differential scales* (interval), respondents are asked to choose their position on a scale between two bipolar words, or range of words or numbers.

- *Evaluative* (good – bad; fresh – stale; cold – hot)
- *Potency* (strong – weak)
- *Activity* (active – passive; tense – relaxed)

The semantic differential results are often displayed as below:

SEMANTIC DIFFERENTIAL SCALE EXAMPLE

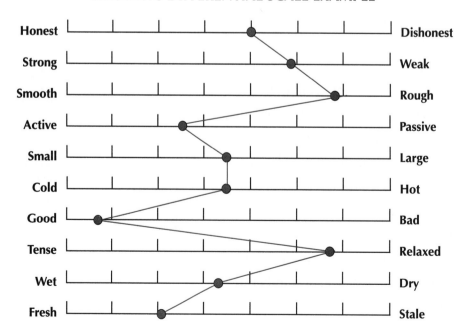

Likert scales (interval) are commonly used to analyze the amount of agreement or disagreement. A Likert item is a statement that the respondent is asked to evaluate according to a subjective or objective criteria, generally the level of agreement or disagreement. For example:

I feel like I belong to this school

Strongly Disagree	Disagree	Neither Agree nor Disagree	Agree	Strongly Agree

Several kinds of response options may be used with a Likert scale. The response option chosen depends upon the purpose for using the questionnaire and the types of questions desired. For the majority of questionnaires, five-point options are recommended. Possible labels include—

- *Endorsement:* strongly disagree, disagree, neutral, agree, strongly agree

- *Frequency:* never, almost never, sometimes, very often, always

- *Intensity:* really apprehensive, somewhat apprehensive, mixed feelings, somewhat excited, really excited

- *Influence:* big problem, moderate problem, small problem, very small problem, no problem

- *Comparison:* much less than others, less than others, about the same as others, more than others, much more than others; much worse than others, worse than others, no difference, better than others, much better than others

Each scale implies how it can be analyzed. Equal interval scales can be averaged. The others must be displayed as frequency distributions or summed in bar graphs. Please note that if more than one scale is used in a questionnaire, the results will need to be analyzed separately—in other words, questions with different scales will probably need to be graphed separately. An often-neglected but very important factor that must be taken into consideration when establishing a scale and format for a questionnaire is the age and attention span of the respondent. Young children do best with two or three response options—smiling faces versus frowning faces. Adults will not finish a questionnaire that requires over thirty minutes of their time.

The example questionnaires provided in the Appendix utilize a five-point endorsement scale. Each item is presented as a declarative sentence, followed by response options that indicate varying degrees of agreement with the statement—from *strongly disagree* to *strongly agree*. The questionnaires go from *strongly disagree* to *strongly agree* because it is our opinion that this direction is left to right—the way Western brains work. That is also why our response options are to the right of the questions.

People often ask about the center option. They worry that most individuals will just use the middle response option if it is made available. Our years of experience with thousands of questionnaires show that people do not automatically choose the middle response. If participants commit to responding to the questionnaire, they will typically respond with precision. When responses on a questionnaire do appear in the middle, the questionnaire constructor needs to examine the questions to determine if it is causing indecision, if the response option and the statement do not go well together, or if, indeed, the respondent does not have a definite response to the question. One of the first things to check is whether there is a conjunction or an adverb in the statement that would cause people to say: *Well, I agree with this part of the question, but I disagree with that part of the question.* Researchers often add the middle response to give respondents a legitimate response option for opinions that are divided or neutral. If you prefer to force your respondents to make a decision, you can always use an even-point scale that has no middle point. You will not be able to average the responses if you do this because you will no longer have an equal interval scale. We add that middle-response option because we think it is a reasonable response option, and because it creates an interval scale giving us the ability to average. We want to graph all the item averages together to show relationships.

Education for the Future has piloted many different scales, including 100, 10, 7, 6, 5, 4, and 3-point scales. We ultimately and easily chose a five-point scale. Any scale that had more than five points upset the respondents—it was too fine a distinction, too hard for participants to respond to. Respondents give us less information and do not complete the questionnaire when they do not like the response options. The even-numbered scales did not allow us to average the responses. Averaging provides the easiest understanding of the relationship of the items to each other. The even-numbered scales did not allow respondents to give a response that indicated half the time "yes" and half the time "no," or "just do not have an opinion at this time." The three-point scale did not discriminate enough.

What about offering *don't know* or *not applicable* as a response option? Some researchers say that *don't know* does not affect the proportion of responses. Depending upon the question, a *not applicable* response might give you more information than getting no response. *Education for the Future* typically does not use either of these options because we want to average the results. We feel these options "mess-up" the scale. Also, in our question construction and piloting phase, we make sure the items are "appropriate" to the respondents.

How Many Response Categories Should an Item Have?

In short, if you want to notice subtle differences in your analyses, your item options will need to discriminate among responses. Consider these questions about the items you put together:

◆ How many response options does it take to discriminate meaningfully?

◆ How many response options will confuse or bore respondents?

◆ Presented with many response options, will respondents use only those responses that are multiples of five, for instance, reducing the number of options anyway?

Write Effective Open-Ended Questions

Effective open-ended questions provide texture and deeper insight into the scaled questions that make up the main body of the questionnaire. Placed at the end of a questionnaire, open-ended questions give respondents a chance to provide additional information that might not have been included in the scaled items.

During the pilot phase, open-ended questions allow questionnaire developers to understand more about how to go about getting their questionnaire information. Piloted open-ended questions can, ultimately, become multiple-choice items.

Effective open-ended questions provide texture and deeper insight into the scaled questions that make up the main body of the questionnaire.

At the core of a good open-ended question is its blunt and general nature, as well as the ability to approach that question with no preconceived notions. If you already have a list of five possible answers to your question, just ask it as a multiple-choice question within the main body of the questionnaire. Plan to listen to the answers to your open-ended questions with an open mind, and be willing to act on the information that has been collected.

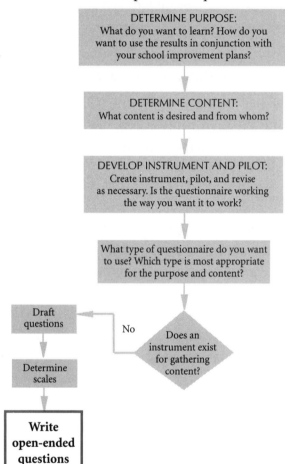

Effective open-ended questions often appear in pairs and give a chance for the respondent to provide positive feedback as well as comments regarding improvement. Any more than three open-ended questions is too many. A good example of the dual approach is asking:

- *What are the strengths of this school?*
- *What needs to be improved in this school?*

or

- *What do you like about this school?*
- *What do you wish were different?*

Providing a simple open-ended question labeled "comments" does not offer enough framing for the respondent to supply structured feedback. Asking clear questions, and using the dual approach illustrated above, will result in feedback that is well constructed and able to be used for action and improvement.

Create the Form

Appearance and arrangement of the questionnaire frequently determine whether respondents will complete it. In fact, research shows that individuals determine within five seconds whether or not they will respond to a questionnaire. Think about what would get you to commit psychologically to completing a questionnaire and build in those same considerations for your respondents. The good news is that once respondents take the effort to read and start a questionnaire, they make a psychological commitment to complete it.

Upon first glance, we definitely want the questionnaire to be appealing to the eye. We want it to have white space. We want to keep the questionnaire consistent. Never split questions, instructions, or responses from the questions between pages. Use an easy-to-read, equally spaced font for the questions themselves. Avoid italics. Make the questionnaire look professional. We typically want to end the questionnaire by giving each

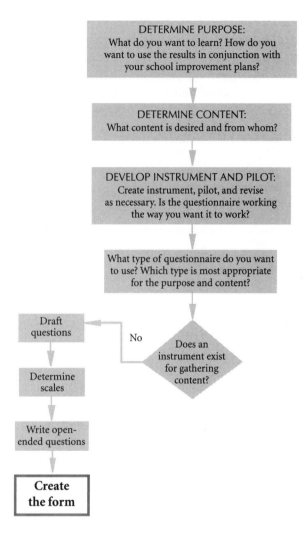

respondent a chance to *comment on the topic*. Figure 3.4-A offers tips to consider when creating the form (as a paper questionnaire). Figure 3.4-B offers tips to consider when writing and placing open-ended questions in a paper questionnaire. Take the time to make the appearance pleasing and the instructions clear to the respondent. Also, take the time to make the questionnaire brain-compatible; written in a common sense, logical fashion as Western brains work, i.e., left-to-right, top-to-bottom. Figures 3.5-A and 3.5-B describe design considerations for online questionnaires.

Figure 3.4-A
DESIGN CONSIDERATIONS FOR MULTIPLE CHOICE PAPER QUESTIONNAIRES

The appearance and arrangement of the questionnaire frequently determine whether or not the respondents will complete it. Try to fit the questions and answers onto one page, if possible. You want the questionnaire to be quick to complete so that the respondent will answer all of the questions.

The majority of Western respondents read from left to right. If the layout of the questions and responses is consistent with this pattern, it will increase the accuracy, and will be easier and faster for respondents to complete.

A clear label shows respondents for whom the questionnaire is intended.

Begin with more general questions and lead up to the more specific.

Write instructions that tell your respondents what you would like them to do.

Leaving white space makes the questionnaire easier to read.

Do not use questions that have conjunctions. Use two separate questions instead.

Ask questions to address the issues that are based on what you want to know, and that cannot be gathered from other sources.

For evidence of school improvement, ask questions that you want to ask over time to see growth.

Think about the impact of every question on your respondent. Make sure the questions will not offend anyone.

Make the questions simple, short, and free of jargon/bureaucratic words.

Avoid:
- trying to assess a little of everything
- leading questions
- jumping around content-wise
- double negatives

Placing response options close to the questions decreases the chance of error due to respondents mismatching lines.

If the questions are worded so that the answers fit into one scale, it will be easier for the respondent to complete and for you to analyze and graph later.

Make it obvious where respondents should make their mark.

Education for the Future

Parents

Please complete this form using a No. 2 pencil. Be sure to completely fill in the circle that describes best what you think or how you feel. Thank you!

PLEASE USE NO. 2 PENCIL.
RIGHT   WRONG

Strongly Disagree / Disagree / Neutral / Agree / Strongly Agree

Question	1	2	3	4	5
I feel welcome at my child's school	①	②	③	④	⑤
I am informed about my child's progress	①	②	③	④	⑤
I know what my child's teacher expects of my child	①	②	③	④	⑤
My child is safe at school	①	②	③	④	⑤
My child is safe going to and from school	①	②	③	④	⑤
There is adequate supervision during school	①	②	③	④	⑤
There is adequate supervision before and after school	①	②	③	④	⑤
Teachers show respect for the students	①	②	③	④	⑤
Students show respect for other students	①	②	③	④	⑤
The school meets the social needs of the students	①	②	③	④	⑤
The school meets the academic needs of the students	①	②	③	④	⑤
The school expects quality work of its students	①	②	③	④	⑤
The school has an excellent learning environment	①	②	③	④	⑤
I know how well my child is progressing in school	①	②	③	④	⑤
I like the school's report cards/progress report	①	②	③	④	⑤
I respect the school's teachers	①	②	③	④	⑤
I respect the school's principal	①	②	③	④	⑤
Overall, the school performs well academically	①	②	③	④	⑤
The school succeeds at preparing children for future work	①	②	③	④	⑤
The school has a good public image	①	②	③	④	⑤
The school's assessment practices are fair	①	②	③	④	⑤
My child's teacher helps me to help my child learn at home	①	②	③	④	⑤
I support my child's learning at home	①	②	③	④	⑤
I feel good about myself as a parent	①	②	③	④	⑤

Children's grades:
- ○ Kindergarten
- ○ First Grade
- ○ Second Grade
- ○ Third Grade
- ○ Fourth Grade
- ○ Fifth Grade
- ○ Sixth Grade
- ○ Seventh Grade
- ○ Eighth Grade
- ○ Ninth Grade
- ○ Tenth Grade
- ○ Eleventh Grade
- ○ Twelfth Grade

Number of children in this school:
① ② ③ ④ ⑤ ⑥ ⑦ ⑧ ⑨

Number of children in the household:
① ② ③ ④ ⑤ ⑥ ⑦ ⑧ ⑨

My native language is:
- ○ Chinese
- ○ Eastern European
- ○ English
- ○ Japanese
- ○ Korean
- ○ Spanish
- ○ Vietnamese
- ○ Other _____

Ethnic background:
(fill in all that apply)
- ○ Black
- ○ American Indian
- ○ Asian
- ○ White
- ○ Hispanic/Latino
- ○ Other _____

Responding:
- ○ Mother
- ○ Father
- ○ Guardian
- ○ Other

Make sure that, however you wish to disaggregate the data later, the information is captured on the form.

In other words, if you want to know the difference between males and females on their responses to particular questions, ask your respondents their gender on the questionnaire.

Figure 3.4-B
DESIGN CONSIDERATIONS FOR MULTIPLE CHOICE PAPER QUESTIONNAIRES

Ask only two to three open-ended questions because of the length of time it takes respondents to reply and because of the difficulty in analyzing the responses. Open-ended questions usually appear at the end of the questionnaire. If all scannable items can be put on one page, place the open-ended on the back.

Place open-ended section at the end of the questionnaire.

Leave enough space for respondents to comment.

Do not use lines. Lines limit feedback. Provide sufficient space for comments—at least two inches.

What are the strengths of your child's school?

What needs to be strengthened at your child's school?

Figure 3.5-A
DESIGN CONSIDERATIONS FOR ONLINE QUESTIONNAIRES

In addition to the same considerations regarding the content of paper questionnaires, we also want online questionnaires to be quick to complete and easy to navigate so that respondents will answer all of the questions.

Customize for the school and type of respondent.

Write a purpose for the questionnaire.

Write instructions that tell the respondents what you would like them to do.

Always thank respondents for taking the questionnaire.

When there is a stem, group few items together. When scrolling, respondents will forget the stem if more than 5 items are in a group.

Set up the questions so respondents read left-to-right.

Do not use questions that have conjunctions. Use two separate questions instead.

If the questions are worded so that the answers fit into one scale, it will be easier for the respondents to complete and for you to analyze and graph later.

Make it obvious where respondents should click on their answer.

(Name Here)Middle School
Staff Questionnaire

This questionnaire is designed to gather general information about what staff members think and feel about the school and their relationship with the school.

In response to the questions asked below, please click on the button next to the answer that is closest to what you think or feel.

Thank you!

I feel:	Strongly Disagree	Disagree	Neutral	Agree	Strongly Agree
like I belong at this school	○	○	○	○	○
that the staff cares about me	○	○	○	○	○
that learning can be fun	○	○	○	○	○
that learning is fun at this school	○	○	○	○	○

I feel:	Strongly Disagree	Disagree	Neutral	Agree	Strongly Agree
recognized for good work	○	○	○	○	○
intrinsically rewarded for doing my job well	○	○	○	○	○
clear about what my job is at this school	○	○	○	○	○
that others are clear about what my job is at this school	○	○	○	○	○

I work with people who:	Strongly Disagree	Disagree	Neutral	Agree	Strongly Agree
treat me with respect	○	○	○	○	○
listen if I have ideas about doing things better	○	○	○	○	○

Figure 3.5-B
DESIGN CONSIDERATIONS FOR ONLINE QUESTIONNAIRES

If you want, you may add two open-ended questions to the questionnaire after the multiple-choice questions and before the demographic options. The response box should expand so those who want to write a lot can do so.

What are the strengths of this school?

What needs to be improved?

DEMOGRAPHIC DATA
For each item, please select the description that applies to you.
These demographic data are used for summary analyses;
some descriptions will not be reported if groups are so small
that individuals can be identified.

Do not use certain demographics if individuals can be identified (i.e., some demographic groups might be so small they would identify individuals)

I am:
(fill in all that apply)
- ☐ African-American
- ☐ American Indian
- ☐ Asian
- ☐ Caucasian
- ☐ Hispanic/Latino
- ☐ Other

I am a(n):
- ○ classroom teacher
- ○ instructional assistant
- ○ certificated staff (other than a classroom teacher)
- ○ classified staff (other than an instructional assistant)

Make sure that, however you wish to disaggregate the data later, the information is captured on the form.

In other words, if you want to know the differences among grade levels on their responses to particular questions, ask your respondents the grade level they teach on the questionnaire.

I teach:
- ○ pre K
- ○ primary grades
- ○ upper elementary grades
- ○ middle school grades
- ○ high school grades 9-10
- ○ high school grades 11-12

I have been teaching:
- ○ 1-3 years
- ○ 4-6 years
- ○ 7-10 years
- ○ 11 or more years

Review and Revise Your Instrument

Examine the content in relation to the other steps in the process: type of questionnaire, type of questions, scaling, respondents, the potential data analysis and presentation of results. Revise to the best of your abilities. Have others carefully review the questionnaire and then revise again as necessary.

DETERMINE PURPOSE:
What do you want to learn? How do you want to use the results in conjunction with your school improvement plans?

↓

DETERMINE CONTENT:
What content is desired and from whom?

↓

DEVELOP INSTRUMENT AND PILOT:
Create instrument, pilot, and revise as necessary. Is the questionnaire working the way you want it to work?

↓

What type of questionnaire do you want to use? Which type is most appropriate for the purpose and content?

↓

Does an instrument exist for gathering content? — No → Draft questions

↓

Determine scales

↓

Write open-ended questions

↓

Create the form

↓

Review and revise

Pilot the Questionnaire

No matter how many times you review the questionnaire after you construct it, you won't know how the questions will actually be interpreted until you administer them to a small number of respondents in your target group as a pilot test. We highly recommend piloting the questionnaire and analyzing the data to understand if you are asking questions that respondents understand and questions that provide responses that lead to your purpose. We also recommend piloting an already developed questionnaire that you might decide to use to make sure it is doing what you want it to do.

To pilot the questionnaire, you can use one of two approaches. One, organize a small group of respondents who are similar to the larger target group. Administer the questionnaire and analyze the results. Include questions on the pilot questionnaire to help you know if the pilot group understood everything on the questionnaire, if they thought the questions were relevant, if there are other questions they feel you should be asking, if they feel the questionnaire was easy to respond to, and to solicit their general overall comments. Another approach is to administer the questionnaire individually to two or three people from each major demographic

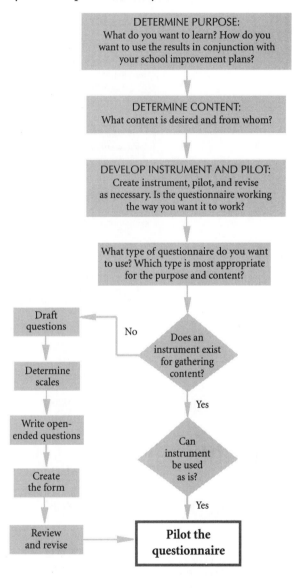

subgroup. Have each person read the items aloud, offer responses, and tell you orally what she/he thinks the question is asking, and what her/his responses mean. This is a very powerful information gatherer *and* quicker than traditional pilot tests. If you are going to use open-ended responses on your questionnaire, be sure to include them as part of the pilot.

Analyze Pilot Results

After you have piloted the questionnaire, look at each of the questions with responses to see if each item was understandable. Look at the open-ended responses for clues to responses that may not seem logical. If respondents are available, ask them to tell you why particular questions were hard to understand.

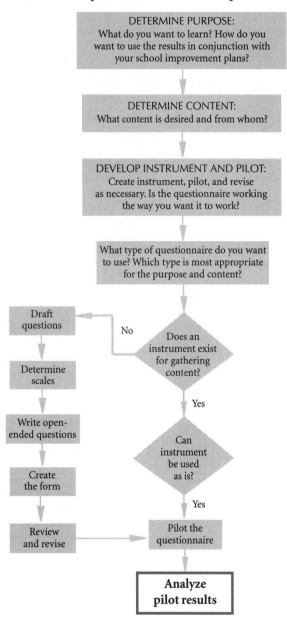

Revise, Review Again, and Finalize

After you study the responses from the pilot group, revise the questionnaire to reflect what you have learned. If you feel that the questions need to be piloted again, do so. It is much better to try out a questionnaire on a different, small group again than to administer a poor questionnaire to a large group. Have several people review the final version of the questionnaire to ensure there are no typographical errors and to ensure that the content flow is as you intend. When you feel that all of the bases have been covered, print the forms or post them online for the "real" questionnaire administration.

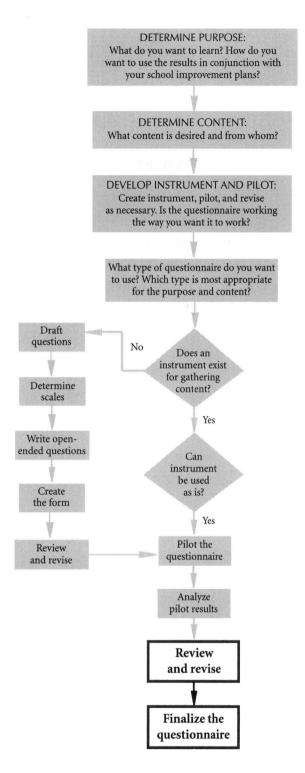

READER CHALLENGE

Do you know what it takes to create a great questionnaire?
Which demographic subgroups are most
important for your questionnaire?

SUMMARY

The development of a questionnaire is critical to the success of the entire questionnaire project. One needs to spend whatever time necessary thinking about purpose, developing appropriate content, questions, scales, piloting the questionnaire, revising, reviewing, and finalizing the instrument to ensure the reliability, validity, and usefulness of the entire questionnaire process.

CHAPTER 4

COLLECTING QUESTIONNAIRE RESPONSES FROM STAFFS, STUDENTS, AND PARENTS

This chapter presents the different methods available for collecting questionnaire responses from staffs, students, and parents; the pros and cons of the different methods; and how to set-up an effective process to administer a questionnaire.

With a good questionnaire in hand, it is time to consider how best to administer it. Figure 4.1 on the next page displays the most common methods of questionnaire data collection in schools, including:

◆ Obtaining responses using paper forms that require hand-entry of responses

◆ Collecting responses using paper scannable forms that are ultimately scanned into a database

◆ Collecting questionnaire responses via the Internet using software that automatically places the responses into a database

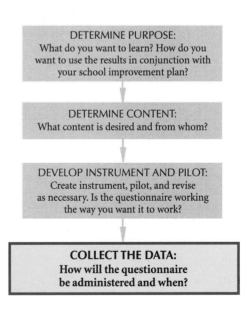

DETERMINE PURPOSE:
What do you want to learn? How do you want to use the results in conjunction with your school improvement plan?

DETERMINE CONTENT:
What content is desired and from whom?

DEVELOP INSTRUMENT AND PILOT:
Create instrument, pilot, and revise as necessary. Is the questionnaire working the way you want it to work?

COLLECT THE DATA:
How will the questionnaire be administered and when?

Figure 4.1
ADMINISTERING THE QUESTIONNAIRE

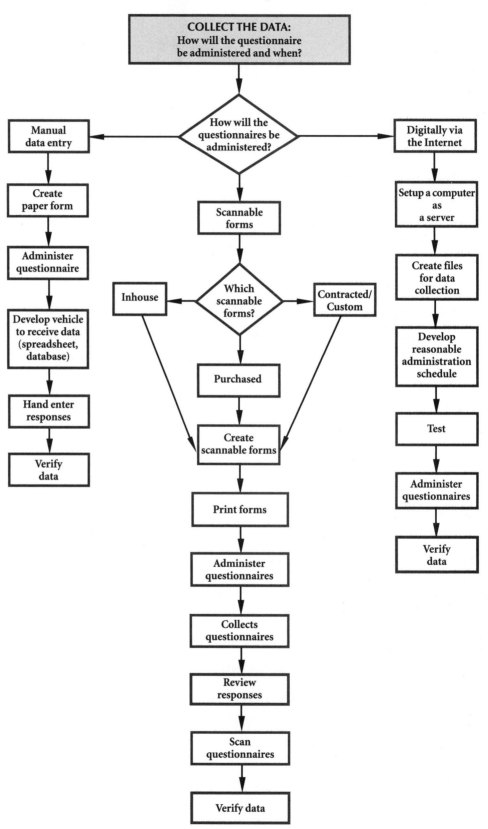

COLLECT THE DATA

Figure 4.2 describes these different data collection options, along with their advantages and disadvantages. No matter what approach is used to collect responses, we recommend moving all data into an electronic environment to facilitate analysis and presentation of the data. An electronic environment provides functions that are unavailable when managing data by hand: statistical functions, disaggregation of data according to demographic subgroups, and formatting the analysis for easy export or pasting into tables or graphs.

Manual Data Entry

Distributing paper questionnaires and manually entering responses into a database or spreadsheet is the least desirable method of data collection. Once data are entered, the spreadsheet or database application will provide analysis capability.

There is no easy way to go about the manual collection and entry of questionnaire data. Depending upon how many questionnaires you have collected, it will consume a significant amount of time which will ultimately impact your ability to turn results around quickly and efficiently for your audience. The time spent in preparing a spreadsheet or database application to receive the entered data is better spent preparing for another method of data collection.

There is one scenario where collecting data by hand can be comprehensive and efficient:

> *ABC School principal wanted to get his school involved in questionnaire work and using data more effectively. The school lacked access to the financial resources and personnel to roll out questionnaires for staffs, parents, and students all at once. The school had undertaken data projects in the past that had not been followed through; and, as a result, the district was less than enthusiastic about adding another ABC School data project to the long list of requirements vying for dollars. This is when entering data by hand made getting questionnaire work done a possibility.*

Distributing paper questionnaires and manually entering responses into a database or spreadsheet is the least desirable method of data collection.

Figure 4.2
DATA COLLECTION OPTIONS

Methods	Advantages	Disadvantages
Manual Data Entry *(Non-scannable Forms)* Once the questionnaire items are finished, the questionnaire form is produced in word processing, database, or desktop publishing software and photocopied or printed. After the forms come back, the responses are manually entered into a database package such as *FileMakerPro* or *Access*, or into a spreadsheet program.	♦ This option requires the least technical expertise and equipment	♦ Time required for data entry and the possibility for human error during the data entry process ♦ If a database is not used, the ability to disaggregate results is essentially lost
In-House Produced Scannable Forms Scannable questionnaires can be produced in-house and printed on a laser printer or sent to a commercial printer for mass copying. This option requires the knowledge and use of a software package that will create a master digital file that is either sent out of the office (off-site) to be printed on an offset printing press or printed to an in-house laser printer.	♦ Producing the form can be done faster than contracting the job out ♦ Can accommodate small groups on a cost-effective basis ♦ Scanning the forms is much faster than manual data entry	♦ Scannable questionnaires can be expensive to produce ♦ Technically challenging ♦ In-house printers are often not consistent enough ♦ Not all commercial printers can print them correctly ♦ If the printing is not calibrated, the form will not be scannable
Purchased Scannable Forms Companies such as Scantron and NCS offer stock scannable (bubble) forms for purchase. You need to add the questions. Some forms allow you to write the questions on the form. Others require the use of two sheets of paper—one for the questions and another sheet for the answers.	♦ Forms are readily available	♦ Somebody has to ensure that all the equipment used is compatible—one cannot just create a scannable form and expect it to work ♦ Resorting to two sheets is not brain compatible ♦ Can be expensive
Contracted Custom Scannable Forms Scannable questionnaires can be roughly designed and sent to companies like Scantron or NCS for final production. This option takes the most time; however, it is a good option on a per-unit basis when there is adequate lead time and large numbers of forms are needed.	♦ Contracting companies usually guarantee that all forms will scan properly ♦ No need for in-house expertise in publishing design ♦ Scanning the forms is much faster than manual data entry	♦ Generally takes from six to eight weeks to have the forms produced ♦ Not a cost-effective option for small numbers
Digital Data Collection A questionnaire can be put online very quickly using an online database such as FilemakerPro, Access, or Sequel Server, or a packaged questionnaire program.	♦ No paper—no printing or distribution costs ♦ Questionnaires can be modified for different groups at minimal cost ♦ People tend to "write" more in response to open-ended questions ♦ Opportunities for human error in scanning or manual data entry are eliminated ♦ Data are available immediately ♦ Responses are automatically converted to electronic/ numeric data	♦ Expertise required in-house or contracted technical expertise and related equipment ♦ Some parents are reluctant to complete online questionnaires

With minimal resources, you can administer questionnaires to your staff members manually and then model the proper use of content, analysis, and presentation. You can show staffs how powerful the data can be, and use that momentum to garner support for a more efficient method of data collection for the larger student and parent populations.

Collect Data With Scannable Forms

Collecting questionnaire data with scannable forms is far more efficient than entering data by hand, but this method still carries with it some administrative oversight and added cost.

After paper questionnaires are designed, printed, and distributed to respondents, the completed questionnaires are run through an optical mark read (OMR) scanner (not the type for scanning photos) that is connected to a computer, where a tab-delimited file of your data is created. (*Tab delimited* means that values are separated by tabs in the file. Values could also be delimited by colons or commas.)

The general steps in working with scannable forms are—

> *Step 1: Create scannable forms.* Purchase scannable forms or design in-house using specific software applications.

> *Step 2: Print forms.* Print forms in-house or send to a professional printer experienced in producing scannable forms (see *Scannable Form Options* in Figure 4.2).

> *Step 3: Administer forms to respondents.*

> *Step 4: Collect forms.*

> *Step 5: Review forms.* Before scanning, review completed forms to ensure that bubbles have been filled in correctly, that erasures have not left extraneous marks, etc.

> *Step 6: Scan forms.* Run completed scannable forms through an optical mark read scanner connected to a computer running a "scanning solution" file created by form-scanning software. The scanning solution file tells the scanner where to look on the page for bubbled-in responses and the

Collecting questionnaire data with scannable forms is far more efficient than entering data by hand, but this method still carries with it some administrative oversight and added cost.

numeric value that should be assigned to each bubble. As a result, a tab-delimited file containing your data is created by the scanning solution.

Step 7: Verify data. Scanned data should be verified to ensure integrity (i.e., that it is a complete sample, that all bubbles have been scanned correctly) before analysis takes place. Import your data file into a database or other application to visually examine the results. This often involves checking the questionnaires against the database record one-by-one. It is time consuming, but well worth the effort considering the importance of the data you are collecting.

Scanning Software and Hardware

Form creation and scanning can take place in two ways—build the capacity to create and scan your own forms, or have an outside organization do the work for you.

The hardware and software used with questionnaire forms are quite different from the hardware and software used for image or photograph scanning, so they are not interchangeable.

The hardware and software used with questionnaire forms are quite different from the hardware and software used for image or photograph scanning, so they are not interchangeable.

Form creation software allows you to design forms with questions and response options aligned on the same page while adhering to strict layout requirements necessary for the scanning process. Form creation software may also be used to gather the results for analysis. Necessary hardware is a PC or Mac computer joined to a printer capable of printing according to exact specifications.

Form scanning hardware involves the use of an optical mark read scanner connected to a computer (PC or Mac) running a scanning solution software application. The completed form is fed into the scanner with the results showing up on the computer file. The structure for this file is often created during the form design process. Companies typically offer one suite of form creation and scanning software. Various models of scanners are available depending upon factors such as dual-side read capacity, ink-read reading capability, auto form feed options, and scanning speed. Scantron (*www.scantron.com*) or NCS (*www.pearsonncs.com*), two of the larger companies that deal with form scanning hardware and software, can provide more specific information.

Producing and Printing Scannable Forms

Scannable forms are often explained as sheets of graph paper, very specific quadrants within a grid (not visible on the form) that are able to collect and place information. In order to scan data into the computer correctly, the forms and the scanner must be lined up perfectly with each other, and marks along the side of the scannable form that tell the scanner where to look for data must be aligned and printed within tight boundaries.

Below are a few notes concerning producing and printing scannable forms:

- *Printing your own forms in-house is not always a good idea.* The number of sheets of paper in the feed tray, how your printer pulls paper through the printer, and paper thickness can all impact the accuracy of your forms. Print in small runs and test-scan your forms frequently to help reduce the potential for problems if you decide to print the forms in-house.

- *A professional print shop can help ensure that your forms will scan properly, but not all print shops can produce scannable forms.* Printing scannable forms requires great attention to detail, as well as advanced equipment. Form creation software will contain support documentation that you can share with your print contractor.

- *Test, test, test—even if you use a professional printer.* The worst-case scenario is that you have a large run of scannable forms printed and they fail to scan correctly. Pull forms from different points in the print run and test scan them.

- Major companies like *Scantron* will produce scannable forms for you and guarantee that they will scan properly.

Collecting Responses Via the Internet

The most efficient and effective method of administering questionnaires is online through an Internet server.

The most efficient and effective method of administering questionnaires is online through an Internet server. With online questionnaires, respondents visit a website that uses form submission web pages that funnel response data to a database or other container for data housed on a server. With online questionnaires, the data collection process is streamlined for a variety of reasons:

◆ Paper is eliminated, as are the administrative oversight and other costs associated with the use of paper.

◆ Most schools and districts already have the hardware and software necessary to administer online questionnaires.

◆ A district can administer questionnaires and monitor the entire process for all of its schools from a single location.

◆ Administrative oversight is minimal. Communication can take place through e-mail.

◆ Duplication of effort is minimized. Files set up for administering questionnaires can be used as templates for data collection and analysis, requiring minimal setup time especially when used with multiple schools.

◆ The costs associated with administering questionnaires depend less on the number of responses, as opposed to using scannable forms, hand-entry, or online methods. Receiving 50 or 500 responses online does not significantly impact time spent in analysis.

◆ Responses are converted to numeric data at the same time that they are submitted to the server. Results can be turned around as soon as the last respondent completes her/his submission.

◆ Questionnaires are administered within a controlled environment, such as a computer lab, to ensure that responses are valid.

◆ Checking the reliability of submissions is streamlined as responses are collected within a structured database environment. The responses are visually easy to check.

- Open-ended responses are collected in the server database and are easily exported to text documents. With paper, you must type each open-ended response to analyze and report the results.

- The technology and files used for online questionnaire administration can be retasked and used for other data collection projects.

Models for Collecting Data Online

Generally speaking, Internet-based data models fall into two categories:

The static data model where data are collected using the Internet, and no calculated result is immediately provided to the respondent. Individuals submit responses to the server and data are accessed or pulled for analysis after the last person has submitted. The most appropriate scenarios for using the static data model occur when the data set is not considered complete for analysis until the last person has participated.

The dynamic data model where data are submitted to the server via the Internet, and a corresponding or calculated result is presented to the respondent of either her/his results alone, or her/his results analyzed with the larger group. Data are dynamically available in order to satisfy requests for the generation of analyses immediately.

The type of model used will have serious implications on the resources required to carry out your project. A static data model requires fewer resources than a dynamic data model. A static model requires less expensive hardware and software and can be carried out by those without much experience with technology. If you can create simple web pages, you can create simple static form submission pages. Creating dynamic, interactive data web pages requires a significant investment in hardware, software, and the personnel to oversee design and maintenance.

The type of model used will have serious implications on the resources required to carry out your project.

For most purposes, the static data model will facilitate questionnaire work very well and will be our focus from this point forward as we discuss the specifics of collecting data via the Internet.

Setting Up Questionnaires Online

Most of the technology to set up questionnaires already exists and just needs local expertise to bring it all together to get the analyses we want. The steps follow:

Most of the technology to set-up online questionnaires already exists and just needs local expertise to bring it all together to get the analyses we want in the end.

Step 1: Set up a computer as a server.

An Internet-based questionnaire server needs:

- *Hardware:* You need a computer to collect questionnaire data online. You don't need to use a computer that is specifically marketed as a server. Any computer will do.

- *Software:* You need server software as well as an application that can organize questionnaire responses. Web serving applications, such as IIS or Apache, are often bundled or included with standard versions of operating systems (Windows XP/Vista, Mac OS X). Common database applications, such as Access or Filemaker Pro, can be used to collect questionnaire responses as numeric data. You can use proprietary survey software, although sometimes your analysis options are limited.

- *Network:* You need to give your computer/server a web address. Contact your network administrator for more information.

Step 2: Create the necessary files to collect data and organize them for administration.

Questionnaire data are easily collected online by using a combination of Internet form submissions pages and database files. The web files (html, php, asp, etc.) allow you to create websites for your questionnaires to which respondents submit responses using a form embedded in the website. The responses go in to a database file that resides on the server but is not seen by respondents.

Using Service Providers to Collect Data Via the Internet

Many service providers allow you to build and administer data collection tools from their websites for a fee. Commercial sites can streamline data collection by providing a structured process to set up questionnaires and collect responses. There may be limits on how you design your site, allow access for submissions, analyze the results, and present the results. Many commercial sites encode the responses collected in their proprietary file formats that can make it difficult to move data into other applications. In the end, creating your own sites and databases for questionnaire administration provides you with greater control over the content, process, and product.

Select the Method of Administration that Will Achieve the Highest Response Rate

The choice among manual entry, scannable form, or online data collection should ultimately be made based on which method will help you realize the highest response rate for each of your respondent groups. Generally speaking, staffs and students are captive audiences and can submit their questionnaire responses online. If parent responses cannot be collected online on site, scannable forms can be sent home with students. Hand entry of data should be chosen only as a last resort, perhaps when the resources are not available to collect the data using any other method.

What Is an Adequate Sample?

How many people do we need to respond to our questionnaire for the results to be considered valid?

Let's think first about the purpose of the questionnaire and why you might sample. To whom you send your questionnaire has to be dependent upon your purpose for doing the questionnaire in the first place. If one reason is to find out what all of your parents are thinking about your school, you will want to send the questionnaire to every parent. Look for the win-wins. You could receive parents' perceptions of the school; and, at the same time, you could be informing them about things that are going on—building your public relations.

One important question to answer before sampling is *will the people who are supposed to use the questionnaire results accept a sample? Education for the Future* seldom uses a sample because of this issue. If all students, parents, and teachers are questioned, the results are compelling. When administering parent, staff, and student questionnaires related to climate perceptions, our goal is 100% participation from each of our respondent groups. Getting 100% participation is easier to realize for students and staffs, and sometimes

Creating your own sites and databases for questionnaire administration provides you with a greater control over the content, process, and product.

Hand entry of data should be chosen only as a last resort.

more difficult with parent groups; but 100% participation is always the goal. We want total "buy in" for the results; we do not want the school community to discount the results because they were drawn from a limited sample.

We also want the results to be used by staffs. To be used effectively, the results must adequately illustrate what is being done well as well as what could be done better. Let's examine the following classroom scenario and determine how sampling might impact our ability to provide results that can be used effectively by staffs:

Getting 100% participation is easier to realize for students and staffs, and sometimes more difficult with parent groups; but 100% participation is always the goal.

> *A teacher has 30 students in her sixth-grade class. Each year it seems that she has three or four "squeaky wheel" parents that take up the bulk of her time, demand the most attention, and manage to make their feedback heard the loudest. She would like to devote more time to communicating with all parents, providing all families with appropriate amounts of attention, and paying attention to feedback from all. To be able to meet her goals, she would like to find out what she is doing well, and apply what she is doing in those areas to what she could be doing better.*

If we take only a small sample of parents from the school, we are more likely to either include all of the squeaky wheels, or not include them at all. We may hear from one particular grade level over another, or from those who have an advantage in responding through language, literacy, or access to technology. What our teacher needs to hear is feedback from all of her parents in order to see what she is doing well and what she could be doing better, and how she can apply what has satisfied most other parents with her "squeaky wheel" parents.

Practically speaking, setting up a sample and ensuring its reliability within a school environment would be more work than what it would take to simply get 100% participation from our staffs, students, and parents. By applying the right technology and establishing an efficient administration process, we can obtain feedback from the entire school community. In the end, drawing from all possible respondents makes the results of our questionnaire work much more powerful.

As we work through the rest of this chapter, our orientation will be that we are always striving for 100% participation, even if this is more difficult to realize for some groups (parents) than for others (students and staffs).

What About Mailing Questionnaires?

Mailing questionnaires, while often seen as a way to get parent responses, is the least desirable way to collect perception data within schools. Mailing questionnaires requires a significant monetary and administrative commitment with no guarantee of return, and no way to appropriately track respondents and follow up with those who have not responded. Return time for mailed questionnaires depends upon those responding and often drags the questionnaire process well beyond projected timelines. Questionnaires need to be routinely resent sometimes up to three times, still resulting with a 30% response rate. School populations are better served with the more structured online or scannable form data collection methods.

Mailing questionnaires, while often seen as a way to get parent responses, is the least desirable way to collect perception data within schools.

Setting Up a Data Collection Process that Makes Sense

Step 1: Communicate the Purpose, Procedures, and Content to Stakeholders Well in Advance

In order for any data work to be successful, the purpose, procedures, and content must be clearly communicated to stakeholders well before data collection begins. Anticipating and answering all of the what, why, when, where, and how questions will go a long way toward helping you obtain a high response rate with honest responses.

When collecting data online, the easiest way to communicate about your questionnaire project is to set up a demonstration site on your server. The demonstration site can consist of a general information page that contains links to demo versions of each of the questionnaires that you will be administering. The general information page can contain information to satisfy the why and when, and the links to demonstration questionnaires can help satisfy the what, where, and how questions. The demonstration sites allow staff members to experience the online method to decrease anxiety about the use of technology, to review the content for each of the questionnaires that will be administered, and to visualize how the respondent groups will submit their responses.

Steps in Setting Up a Data Collection Process

Step 1. *Communicate purpose, procedures, and content to stakeholders*

Step 2. *Select the best time to administer questionnaires*

Step 3. *Select the administration environment*

Step 4. *Establish a manageable administration schedule*

Step 5. *Provide a narrow window of administration for each questionnaire*

Step 6. *Provide additional language access*

Step 7. *Test the data collection tools prior to administration*

Step 8. *Verify the data*

Step 2: Select the Best Time to Administer Questionnaires

There is really no "best" time of year to administer questionnaires (when administering questionnaires that truly measure environmental perceptions). Significant differences are rarely seen in data that are collected in the Fall versus the Spring. It is more important that questionnaires be administered at generally the same time each year, every year.

Questionnaires are administered at generally the same time each year, every year.

If you choose to administer your questionnaires in the Fall, allow enough of the school calendar to pass so that respondents will have adequate experience with the school to inform their responses. If the school year starts in late August, you should not administer your questionnaires before mid October. If you choose to administer your questionnaires in the Spring, be careful not to overwhelm respondents during a time that is heavy with testing.

A key consideration in scheduling your parent questionnaire administration is determining when you are most likely to have parents onsite in large enough numbers that collecting their responses online becomes a viable option. For elementary schools, Fall parent-teacher conferences provide a great opportunity to collect parent responses because these conferences are usually the most highly attended parent-onsite activity of the year. We like to put the students in charge of ushering parents to the computer lab, getting them comfortable with the questionnaire process, and then escorting the parents to their conferences when finished with the questionnaire. For middle or high schools, parent-teacher conferences, curriculum nights, or even athletic/music/drama events might be considered as times to collect parent responses if the opportunity is well publicized.

Step 3: Select the Environment for Administration

A carefully selected environment for completing questionnaires can help facilitate a good return as well as honest responses.

A carefully selected environment for completing questionnaires can help facilitate a good return, honest responses, and can also provide facilitators to provide administrative oversight and assistance.

Staff members can submit their responses in a computer lab setting during a staff meeting; in short order, you have a 100% response rate. An e-mail link can be used for convenience, but then you won't know who did not respond and cannot follow-up with individuals to give them the opportunity to respond. Students and parents can submit their responses in a computer lab as well where large numbers can respond simultaneously, and facilitators can provide oversight and assistance as needed.

Schedule staff questionnaire administration first. In submitting their responses, staff members will become familiar with the process of submitting responses and will be better able to organize and lead students through the process. When students submit their responses, they become equally familiar, and they are then available to help parents with the technology and language. If using scannable forms for parents, students are more likely to take parent questionnaires home and return the completed forms to staff in a timely manner after they have completed their own online submissions.

Step 4: Establish a Manageable Schedule for Administration

With the impact of administration order in mind, use the school calendar to identify a target date for parents (during conferences); schedule students at least a week before parent conferences and staffs at least a week before the student administration.

For school districts facilitating questionnaires for a large number of schools, the timeline for data collection should depend largely upon the amount of oversight and troubleshooting that can be provided by those facilitating data collection. Scheduling questionnaires for every school in a large district for the same week could seriously impact the ability to provide schools with needed oversight and assistance. If facilitators at the district level can effectively communicate with only five schools per week about their student questionnaires, and there are 20 schools in the district, schedule the administration of student questionnaires over a four-week period. Figure 4.3 on the next page is a sample questionnaire administration planning sheet.

Figure 4.3
QUESTIONNAIRE INFORMATION PROJECT PLANNING AND TRACKING FORM

District Name	Kelly River County School District		
Contact Information	Jane Smith	jsmith@grcsd.org	555-555-5555
	CONTACT NAME	CONTACT E-MAIL	CONTACT TELEPHONE NUMBER

ELEMENTARY

	Grades	STUDENTS (3-point Q)				STUDENTS (5-point Q)				STAFF				PARENTS			
		Desired Ns	Date(s)	Online	Paper	Desired Ns	Date(s)	Online	Paper	Desired Ns	Date(s)	Online	Paper	Desired Ns	Date(s)	Online	Paper
Belle Aire	1st - 5th	95	10/20 – 10/24	x		78	10/20 – 10/24	x		30	10/20 – 10/24	x		175	10/24 – 10/28	x	
Cherry Hill	1st - 5th	470	11/3 – 11/7	x		325	11/3 – 11/7	x		72	10/20 – 10/24	x		600	10/24 – 10/28	x	
Eastside	1st - 5th	70	10/27 – 10/31	x		75	10/27 – 10/31	x		28	10/20 – 10/24	x		120	10/24 – 10/28	x	
Rose Avenue	1st - 5th	650	11/3 – 11/7	x			11/3 – 11/7	x		20	10/20 – 10/24	x		780	11/24 – 10/28	x	
Sunnyside	K	680	11/3 – 11/14	x		500	11/3 – 11/14	x		60	10/20 – 10/24	x		795	10/24 – 10/28	x	

MIDDLE

	Grades	STUDENTS (3-point Q)	STUDENTS (5-point Q)				STAFF				PARENTS			
			Desired Ns	Date(s)	Online	Paper	Desired Ns	Date(s)	Online	Paper	Desired Ns	Date(s)	Online	Paper
Eastside Middle	6th - 8th	N/A	1,322	10/20 – 10/24	x		54	10/20 – 10/24	x		1,300	10/20 – 10/24	x	
Kelly River Middle	6th - 8th		1,600	10/20 – 10/24	x		74	10/20 – 10/24	x		1,500	10/20 – 10/24	x	
King Middle	6th - 8th		1,749	10/20 – 10/24	x		78	10/20 – 10/24	x		1,600	10/20 – 10/24	x	

HIGH SCHOOLS

	Grades	STUDENTS (3-point Q)	STUDENTS (5-point Q)				STAFF				PARENTS			
			Desired Ns	Date(s)	Online	Paper	Desired Ns	Date(s)	Online	Paper	Desired Ns	Date(s)	Online	Paper
Eastside High	9th - 12th	N/A	1,822	10/20 – 10/24	x		68	10/24 – 10/24	x	600	1,524	10/20 – 10/28	x	
Kelly River High	9th - 12th		1,907	10/20 – 10/24 if needed 11/5 and 11/6	x		74	10/24 – 10/24	x	600	1,642	10/20 – 10/28 if needed 11/5 and 11/6	x	

Step 5: Provide a Narrow Window of Administration for Each Questionnaire

Selecting a narrow window of administration will help focus your administrative and support efforts and allow you to respond to low response rates or other issues quickly. Opening questionnaire administration to a broad timeline usually decreases the ability to identify exactly who has responded and how to provide additional access or resources.

The window for administration depends largely upon the respondent pool. For students responding online, for instance, it is realistic to allocate a week for the collection of submissions, even at the high school level. Staff and parents may be isolated to a specific event, such as a staff meeting or a parent-teacher conference.

Step 6: Provide Additional Language Access

Providing access to questionnaires in multiple languages can be facilitated online by providing respondents with the opportunity to select from a variety of pages that contain the same questionnaire but in different languages. Each questionnaire page can be submitted to the same database or another resource on the server where the responses are converted to numeric data. For scannable forms, multiple versions of the same form can be produced for each language and, when scanned, can be combined into a single data file for analysis.

Producing the translated content should not be taken lightly. If care and consideration are not taken to acknowledge the colloquial or regional use of the language, the result may be that the process is more exclusive than inclusive.

A larger issue than translation can be access to the technology for data collection for second language groups. Respondents who require assistance with language may be more likely to require assistance in using the technology to submit their responses. A solution is to ask students or staffs who are able to address both the language and technology issues to facilitate questionnaires for respondents.

Respondents who require assistance with language may be more likely to require assistance in using the technology to submit their responses.

Step 7: Test the Data Collection Tools Prior to Administration

A critical part of effectively collecting questionnaire data involves thoroughly testing the tools to be used before releasing them to respondents. For collecting data online, testing involves submitting responses to each of the questionnaire sites. If using scannable forms, pull forms from various points within the print run, fill them out, and run them through the OMR scanner to make sure data are recorded accurately. Any work associated with the testing that is completed before actually collecting data will pale in comparison to the efforts required if you experience problems with online data submission or form scanning.

Step 8: Verify the Data

In verifying the data, consider the number of people who were given the questionnaire and the number of responses received. If the number of responses is low, follow-up with those who received the questionnaire originally to get more responses. If your parent questionnaire was given at parent–teacher conferences and only 60% of your parents attended (identified through a guest book or sign-in sheets in each classroom), you could use another format to get additional responses from the parents who did not attend. Only with in-person administration procedures can you know exactly who responded to an anonymous questionnaire. You could send scannable questionnaires to those who did not attend. Figure 4.4 shows Figure 4.3 completed to document response numbers to ensure the best possible sample.

For each of the approaches to gathering questionnaire data, you will need to verify the accuracy of the data collection.

For each of the approaches to gathering questionnaire data, you will need to verify the accuracy of the data collection. For online data collection, remove any duplicates, tests, or otherwise errant responses from your sample. For scannable forms, recheck the reliability of your scanning process by checking responses from a few of the scannable forms against the data file produced by the scanner.

Figure 4.4
QUESTIONNAIRE INFORMATION RESPONSE DETAIL REPORT

District Name	Kelly River County School District
Date	Fall 2008

ELEMENTARY	STUDENTS (3-point Q)				STUDENTS (5-point Q)				STAFF				PARENTS			
	Desired Ns	10/26	11/3	11/10	Desired Ns	10/27	11/3	11/10	Desired Ns	10/27	11/3	11/10	Desired Ns	10/27	11/3	11/10
Belle Aire Elementary	95	0	22	89	78	0	16	78	30	8	10	28	175	13	136	166
Cherry Hill Elementary	470	90	186	470	325	1	129	321	72	24	24	68	600	19	311	541
Eastside Elementary	70	0	0	70	75	0	16	67	28	9	9	24	120	0	92	120
Rose Avenue Elementary	650	209	209	647					20	6	6	18	780	95	480	698
Sunnyside Elementary	680	222	429	678	500	147	298	490	60	20	28	58	795	140	621	744

MIDDLE	STUDENTS (3-point Q)	STUDENTS (5-point Q)				STAFF				PARENTS			
	N/A	Desired Ns	10/27	11/3	11/10	Desired Ns	10/27	11/3	11/10	Desired Ns	10/27	11/3	11/10
Eastside Middle		1,322	704	1,122	1,309	54	0	36	54	1,300	0	894	1,196
Kelly River Middle		1,600	509	509	509	74	32	64	74	1,500	0	246	1,403
King Middle		1,749	609	1,376	1,739	78	0	58	78	1,600	0	1,146	1,688

HIGH	STUDENTS (3-point Q)	STUDENTS (5-point Q)				STAFF				PARENTS			
	N/A	Desired Ns	10/27	11/3	11/10	Desired Ns	10/27	11/3	11/10	Desired Ns	10/27	11/3	11/10
Eastside High		1,822	0	1,493	1,819	68	0	29	68	1,524	0	495	1,516
Kelly River High		1,907	391	1,249	1,859	74	34	68	74	1,642	33	1,249	1,608

Note: Numbers above do not account for test or duplicate submissions to be removed prior to analysis.

Security and Online Questionnaires

A secure environment for collecting questionnaire data online can be achieved either through technology or by setting up an effective process.

A secure environment for collecting questionnaire data online can be achieved either through technology or by setting up an effective process.

With technology, we can build elaborate systems to validate users with checks such as unique user names and passwords. This technology requires a greater degree of knowledge and experience with technology, and it often results in the transition from a static (simple) data model to a dynamic (complex) model.

In designing an effective process for collecting responses, however, we can achieve a comparable level of security. A few guiding ideas can help facilitate a secure process:

◆ For students and parents, administer questionnaires within a computer lab or other environment where participation can be supervised and support provided as needed. Set the time frame so it is difficult, or impossible, for someone to submit more than one form.

◆ Set up data collection websites for each school, each with its own separate staff, student, and parent questionnaire sites. Respondents can only submit responses for their particular questionnaire for their school. Their responses more readily trackable on the server.

◆ Provide web addresses for access to each questionnaire for each school, and only just before data collection is to take place. Do not provide links to the questionnaires anywhere on the web. By asking respondents to enter a web address into a browser, you are facilitating a degree of validation without having to oversee the distribution of user names and passwords.

◆ Add auto-entering date and time fields to your data collection databases so you can track exactly when submissions were received. Any responses received outside of the agreed administration time period may be suspect.

In the end, simple form submission to a database provides us with the greatest amount of security as databases used for collection (hence the raw data) need not be broadcast directly to the web.

As with other data projects, all data collected must be validated prior to analysis regardless of the safeguards in place prior to collection. The databases used on the server provide a great environment for reviewing and validating our data, which ultimately reduces the need to put technology in place to secure data collection. In the end, a secure process will help us more than focusing on technological solutions that may add complex layers to the work.

All data collected must be validated prior to analysis regardless of the safeguards in place prior to collection.

READER CHALLENGE

How and when will you collect your questionnaire data? What is the desired number of staff members, students, and parents who can respond to the questionnaires for each of your schools?

SUMMARY

The data collection model one decides to use to administer a questionnaire requires careful thought.

Using a website is the most efficient and effective way of administering a questionnaire because most schools and districts already have the necessary hardware and software. Administering questionnaires online also provides quick access to the data that will be analyzed as part of the school improvement process.

The purposes, procedures, and content of the questionnaire must be communicated to stakeholders before the actual data collection process begins. A secure environment must be established, and all data collected must be validated prior to analysis.

CHAPTER **5**

ANALYZING QUESTIONNAIRE DATA

This chapter explains the elements of effective questionnaire analysis and provides an overview of tools to carry out the analysis.

When creating a questionnaire, one needs to make sure the content and design facilitate effective data analysis and effective use of the results. The structure of the questions dictates how the responses will be analyzed and how the results will be presented.

If we want to be able to see all items in relation to each other, all items need to use the same scale and be phrased in the same way (e.g., stated positively). A single scale for all items allows us to analyze responses to all questions along a single point of orientation (scale) and to place the results together in the same graph.

If different scales are used, and if positively and negatively phrased questions are combined in the body of the questionnaire, different methods are required to analyze and present the results. Like-scaled and/or phrased items need to be grouped into

DETERMINE PURPOSE:
What do you want to learn? How do you want to use the results in conjunction with your school improvement plan?

DETERMINE CONTENT:
What content is desired and from whom?

DEVELOP INSTRUMENT AND PILOT:
Create instrument, pilot, and revise as necessary. Is the questionnaire working the way you want it to work?

COLLECT THE DATA:
How will the questionnaire be administered and when?

ANALYZE RESULTS:
How can the results be analyzed to show the information gleaned from the questionnaire?

separate files for analysis of results and into separate graphs for presentation. Sometimes items are different enough that they warrant using different scales and phrasing, but most often content phrasing can be adjusted to the use of a single scale and uniform phrasing. Figure 5.1 breaks down the steps for analyzing the results of the questionnaire.

Figure 5.1
ANALYZING QUESTIONNAIRE RESULTS

```
                  ┌─────────────────────────────────────┐
                  │         ANALYZE RESULTS:            │
                  │ How can the results be analyzed to show the │
                  │ information gleaned from the questionnaire? │
                  └─────────────────────────────────────┘
                                   │
                                   ▼
                              ◇ How will the
                                results be
                                analyzed? ◇
    ┌──────────────┐        ╱        │        ╲        ┌──────────────┐
    │ Spreadsheet  │◀──────            │             ──▶│   Custom     │
    │ application  │                   │                │   database   │
    └──────────────┘                   │                └──────────────┘
           │                           │                       │
           ▼                           ▼                       ▼
    ┌──────────────┐           ┌──────────────┐        ┌──────────────────┐
    │ Develop and  │           │ Statistical  │        │ Create database for│
    │ test formulas│           │ analysis software│     │ each questionnaire │
    │ for analysis │           │ application  │        │ (develop fields,   │
    └──────────────┘           │ (i.e., SPSS) │        │ calculations, and  │
           │                   └──────────────┘        │ scripts for analysis│
           │                           │                └──────────────────┘
           │                           ▼                       │
           └────────────────▶ ┌──────────────┐ ◀──────────────┘
                              │ Analyze scaled-│
                              │ item responses │
                              └──────────────┘
                                     │
                                     ▼
                              ┌──────────────┐
                              │ Analyze open- │
                              │ ended responses│
                              └──────────────┘
                                     │
                                     ▼
                              ┌──────────────┐
                              │   Verify     │
                              └──────────────┘
```

THE SCHOOL/BUILDING AS THE UNIT OF MEASUREMENT

The intent of *Education for the Future* questionnaires is to have school staffs look at themselves through the perceptions of students, staffs, and parents, agree on what they want the school to look and feel like, and then determine what they are going to do to get there.

We believe that each school is unique, with students, staffs, and families of varying backgrounds and experiences, and that the school should not be compared to other schools. We sometimes plot total questionnaire responses from each school in the same graph for district leadership purposes. However, we want leadership to keep in mind the unique and distinct characteristics of each school in the interpretation.

We believe that each school is unique, with students, staffs, and families of varying backgrounds and experiences, and that the school should not be compared to other schools.

ANALYSIS POINTS: BY DEMOGRAPHICS AND BY YEAR

Establish analysis points that can consistently provide useful and valuable information for each school or building. Disaggregate or sort results by demographics, by year, and by other specific characteristics of the group being surveyed to lead deeper and deeper into issues.

Typical analysis descriptions follow:

Analysis of total survey respondents provides a general overview of our questionnaire results. This information plots general differences among items and illustrates some general thematic ties among items.

Analysis by demographic variables allows schools to isolate differences in responses by subgroups within the school population. Looking into general demographic subgroups, such as gender, ethnicity, and grade level, provides valuable information about the perceptions of questionnaire respondents. By selecting demographic variables carefully, schools can tie perception data to demographic, student learning, and school process data to give them a clearer picture of how perceptions/ climate/environment influence learning.

Analysis by year is perhaps the most powerful level of analysis. Looking at changes over time validates the work a school has done and helps staff members realign their actions. It should be noted that strategies for change should not focus on questionnaire results on their own; perception data, along with demographics, student learning, and school process data, can tell the whole story.

When disaggregating or sorting any data for analysis, one needs to take care not to provide analyses where individuals can be identified. Providing any analysis of perception data with subgroups fewer than eight can impact the interpretation of the analysis. Potential risks include alienating questionnaire respondent groups by creating a feeling of negative accountability by identifying individuals, or by having readers put undeserved emphasis on results during interpretation.

Complex Analysis or Simple Statistics?

Descriptive statistics, simple summaries used to explain the basic characteristics of the data, are very powerful for analyzing school perceptions. We want to see items in relationship to each other, and to know if different groups are responding to processes in the same or different ways. In addition, producing average statistics for each item, and then eyeballing the relationship of items to each other, can reveal differences and highlight themes. Schools want to know what they are doing well, what they can do better for students, and to know what actions to take. Descriptive statistics can help schools do all of these.

"Significant differences" determined through complex statistical analyses often cement the differences rather than provide information on which to change. For example, if questionnaire results were "significantly different" for classified staff versus certificated classroom teachers on an item related to the school having a shared vision, it would not inspire all staff to work together to revisit and make the vision shared or even to look at other items. It might be perceived that one group should "get on board."

If descriptive statistics showed that items related to working closely together, sharing decisions, and planning were low, in addition to a shared vision, the whole staff would be more likely to work together to revisit the vision and redefine the major parts, such as sharing decisions, collaboration, and planning.

Avoiding Redundant Analysis

At times it seems that unending streams of analyses can be created. The key is to determine what small percentage of these analyses are actionable, and then decide what can be avoided as redundant. Avoid burying users with analyses that do not prompt them to see their results easily, uncover new

Schools want to know what they are doing well, what they can do better for students, and to know what actions to take. Descriptive statistics can help schools do all of these.

interpretations of the results, or provide further clarification of the results through disaggregations. We want to focus on analyses that get to the point and relay the results effectively.

Perceptions data, unlike other forms of data, may not need to be disaggregated down to multiple subgroups in order to take effective action. Disaggregating the data into smaller and smaller subgroups, beyond grade, gender, and ethnic subgroups, may reinforce what is seen in the more general results.

When creating analyses, ask yourself if the analysis is telling you anything beyond what has already been created, or if it is helping you see the data in a new way. Instead of focusing on presenting analyses that are redundant, it would be better to focus energy into other areas of data, tying the perception data to other measures.

Tools for Creating Effective Analyses

Tools for creating effective analyses range from simple spreadsheet applications to more complex statistical or custom database applications. In addition to ease of use, and perhaps more important, is the impact that the tool can have on the integrity of the data, the standard by which a selection should be made.

As questionnaire data are collected, processed, and presented, they often pass through different tools. As responses move from one "tool" environment to another, referred to as passing through "data thresholds," errors can occur that can impact the integrity of the data.

To our benefit, simple spreadsheet applications can often provide the level of analysis that we need. Spreadsheet applications are common to most desktop computer software installations, and they are familiar to most computer users.

Simple spreadsheet applications can often provide the level of analysis we need.

To our detriment, spreadsheet applications hold data in cells that are readily accessible, which means that data can be edited and moved around easily—sometimes too easily. As we develop calculations to create analyses, the cursor is often dragged and dropped through large amounts of data. This flexibility and functionality can result in data accidentally being moved among fields and analysis formulas.

Also common to the use of spreadsheet applications is the duplication of work. The sizes of data files and the number of fields vary among the different types of questionnaires, so the analysis tasks must be repeated for each questionnaire. Analysis formulas are defined repeatedly, potentially producing errors with the unprotected nature of the data and the duplication of work.

Statistical analysis software applications, such as SPSS (Statistical Package for the Social Sciences, *http://www.spss.com*), provide data security and automated statistical analysis. Analysis features are automated through the use of dialogue boxes, not by dragging and dropping across large files of data.

While providing some automation of analyses through dialogue boxes, statistical applications might require the dialogue box functions to be repeated manually for every dataset brought into the application for analysis. This can sometimes result in repeated work that can be facilitated through push-button scripting, saving time and ensuring that the process is repeated the same each time. The learning curve associated with such functionality can be fairly steep, decreasing turn-around time until the functions are mastered.

More sophisticated analysis is available with statistical applications. While you pay for the full complement of analysis functionality, you might not ever use it to its full capacity. The descriptive statistics described earlier in this chapter make up a very small percentage of the statistical functionality in statistical applications. More analysis capability isn't always better. If you are already using such an application for other data work, using it for perceptions work may be an easy choice. If not, you might want to consider another tool for the job.

The potential for error becomes narrower when using statistical analysis applications, but the analysis applications may be offset by a learning curve with functionality that isn't fully used to its potential in relation to the overall cost.

Database applications written to process perception data provide the best of all worlds.

Database applications written to process perception data provide the best of all worlds. They provide a safe and secure environment for data, decreasing the direct interaction with the response data once they are brought in for analysis. Calculations and analysis functionality can be designed to accomplish specific tasks. Without filtering through a myriad of functions to find what is useful; simply determine what is useful ahead of time and program the functionality directly. Analysis processes can be scripted into the single push of a button. No need to repeat analysis steps over and over with each dataset you wish to analyze. Small-scale database applications (such as *FileMaker* or *Access*) are readily accessible and less expensive than statistical analysis applications, and these small-scale database applications are often bundled as part of a desktop computer purchase or with an office suite of applications.

Of course, there is a downside to database applications. You need to know how to write one, or have the resources to employ someone who knows how. In their construction, database applications are far more complex than using a spreadsheet or statistical analysis application. The good news is that the functionality in a database application needs to be written only once, and then it can be retasked for other uses. You may be able to find database developers online who share their applications readily. This means that you can copy and use the functionality that you want without having to create the applications from scratch.

In the end, the best advice is to use a small-scale database application if you can, use a statistical analysis application if you already use one for other data work, and use a spreadsheet application only if you absolutely have to.

ANALYZING OPEN-ENDED RESPONSES

Open-ended questions should not be overlooked when assessing perceptions of the learning environment. The responses to open-ended questions, such as *What are the strengths of this school?* and *What needs to be improved?* provide a very rich context for interpreting the questions in the body of a questionnaire. Just as with the responses for the scaled items, we want to learn what we are doing well along with what we could be doing better so that we can take action based on the results presented.

Open-ended questions should not be overlooked when assessing perceptions of the learning environment.

The first component of analyzing open-ended responses effectively is approaching the work with an open mind and not a set of preconceived notions. We ask open-ended questions because we want to hear from our respondents, not because we want to validate a list of keywords or items that we think will appear in the open-ended responses.

There is no fast or automated way to analyze open-ended responses. Because we do not approach open-ended responses with a predetermined list of responses, we do not use text or other open-ended response analysis software that isolates and counts certain keywords within the open-ended responses. To process open-ended responses properly, read through them individually, and aggregate them when possible using your own discretion to decide when to collapse or reduce responses to phrases or single words. Review the responses and add up the number of times respondents said the same thing. (See Figure 5.2) Place the number, in parentheses, after the statement, eliminate the duplicates, and revise your list. For example, *I like the caring teachers and the friendly school, I like that our school is new and the teachers are nice,* and *I really like our new principal and my friends* can be collapsed to:

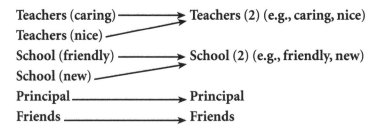

> *While open-ended responses to questions are very time-consuming to compile or aggregate, this work is critical to understanding and taking action on the data that have been collected.*

While open-ended responses to questions are very time-consuming to compile or aggregate, this work is critical to understanding the respondents' thinking reflected in the multiple choice answers.

Different methods of data collection facilitate the analysis of open-ended responses differently. If you collect responses using scannable forms, you will need to type the open-ended responses from each form. If you collect your questionnaire responses via the Internet, the typed-in comments are collected in a database file and open-ended responses can be isolated and exported directly to a text document for review and aggregation.

Figure 5.2
AGGREGATING OPEN-ENDED RESPONSES

All Responses

I like the caring teachers and the friendly school

I like that our school is new and the teachers are nice

I have a good teacher and friends who treat me nice

I like the way teachers make us learn things

I feel safe and treated with respect from teachers

I like my teacher and the principal

My teacher treats me with respect

I like my friends and my nice teacher

I really like our new principal and my friends

We have a nice school

I like recess, social studies, P.E., and music

I like recess and the slide and the swings

I like reading and music and math

Not too much homework

Eliminate Duplicates, Add Descriptors, and Rank Order

Aggregated Responses

The teachers (8) (e.g., nice, 2; respect/fair, 2; caring, 1; good, 1; way of learning, 1)

The school (3) (e.g., friendly, 1; new, 1; nice, 1)

My friends (3) (e.g., treat me nice, 1)

Music (2),

My classes (2)

The principal (2)

Recess (2) (e.g., playground equipment, 1)

Not too much homework

Social Studies, Math, P.E., Reading

Interpretation and aggregation of the open-ended responses can become a professional learning activity to be carried out at the school site as a follow-up to interpretation of the graphed results.

The reality of good open-ended work is that it requires time and effort, and sometimes can have an impact on how effectively the results are used. In many cases, interpretation and aggregation of the open-ended responses can become a professional learning activity to be carried out at the school site as a follow-up to interpretation of the graphed results. Staff members can review the graphed results, note themes, and then examine the open-ended responses to draw any correlations. Professional learning with respect to open-ended results at the site level can become creative, with teams reviewing responses and creating 'top ten' lists or other ways to present the results to the group and spark a discussion of the findings.

READER CHALLENGE

List the applications currently licensed by your school district that can help you complete the analysis portion of your project.

SUMMARY

Questionnaires are administered to provide information about student, staff, and parent perceptions of the learning environment. To be useful, the results must be understandable and provide a guide for improvement.

The content and design of the questionnaire should facilitate effective analysis and use of the results.

Determining which tools to use for analysis is vital since it is through the analysis and use of perceptions of staff members, students, and parents results that school improvement can begin.

CHAPTER **6**

PRESENTING
QUESTIONNAIRE RESULTS

This chapter explains how effective presentation of questionnaire results allows respondents and others to see the big picture, understand what needs to improve, and what action to take. This chapter also discusses tools that efficiently present perception data results for effective use.

We want to present questionnaire results in a way that facilitates easy interpretation, provides contextual understanding, and creates a "Wow!" moment with data. We know that teachers do not have the time to analyze or use complex questionnaire results. It behooves the preparers of the results to forego complex analyses and to reduce large amounts of information to a single or a small number of graphs that provide powerful information, and to provide a report summarizing the information. The power of graphs comes from their ability to convey data directly to the viewer. Viewers use spatial intelligence to retrieve data from a graph—a source different from the language-based intelligence of prose and verbal presentations.

REPORT RESULTS

Questionnaires are designed to ask multiple questions to understand the "Big Picture" while defining what needs to improve to get better results.

Questionnaires are designed to ask multiple questions to understand the "Big Picture" while defining what needs to improve to get better results. Figure 6.1 shows the steps reporting questionnaire results.

We are all used to seeing questionnaire results as presented in Figure 6.2 (page 88). When results are presented in this manner, it is very hard to know which items are most important, highest, or lowest. We don't even think about how the items might work together. It is just too confusing. When using results from this type of presentation, most people pick just one or two items to work on. Even worse, people might ignore them all, especially if they don't understand the *Big Picture*.

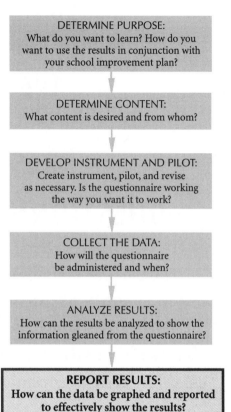

DETERMINE PURPOSE:
What do you want to learn? How do you want to use the results in conjunction with your school improvement plan?

DETERMINE CONTENT:
What content is desired and from whom?

DEVELOP INSTRUMENT AND PILOT:
Create instrument, pilot, and revise as necessary. Is the questionnaire working the way you want it to work?

COLLECT THE DATA:
How will the questionnaire be administered and when?

ANALYZE RESULTS:
How can the results be analyzed to show the information gleaned from the questionnaire?

REPORT RESULTS:
How can the data be graphed and reported to effectively show the results?

Figure 6.1
REPORTING QUESTIONNAIRE RESULTS PROCESS

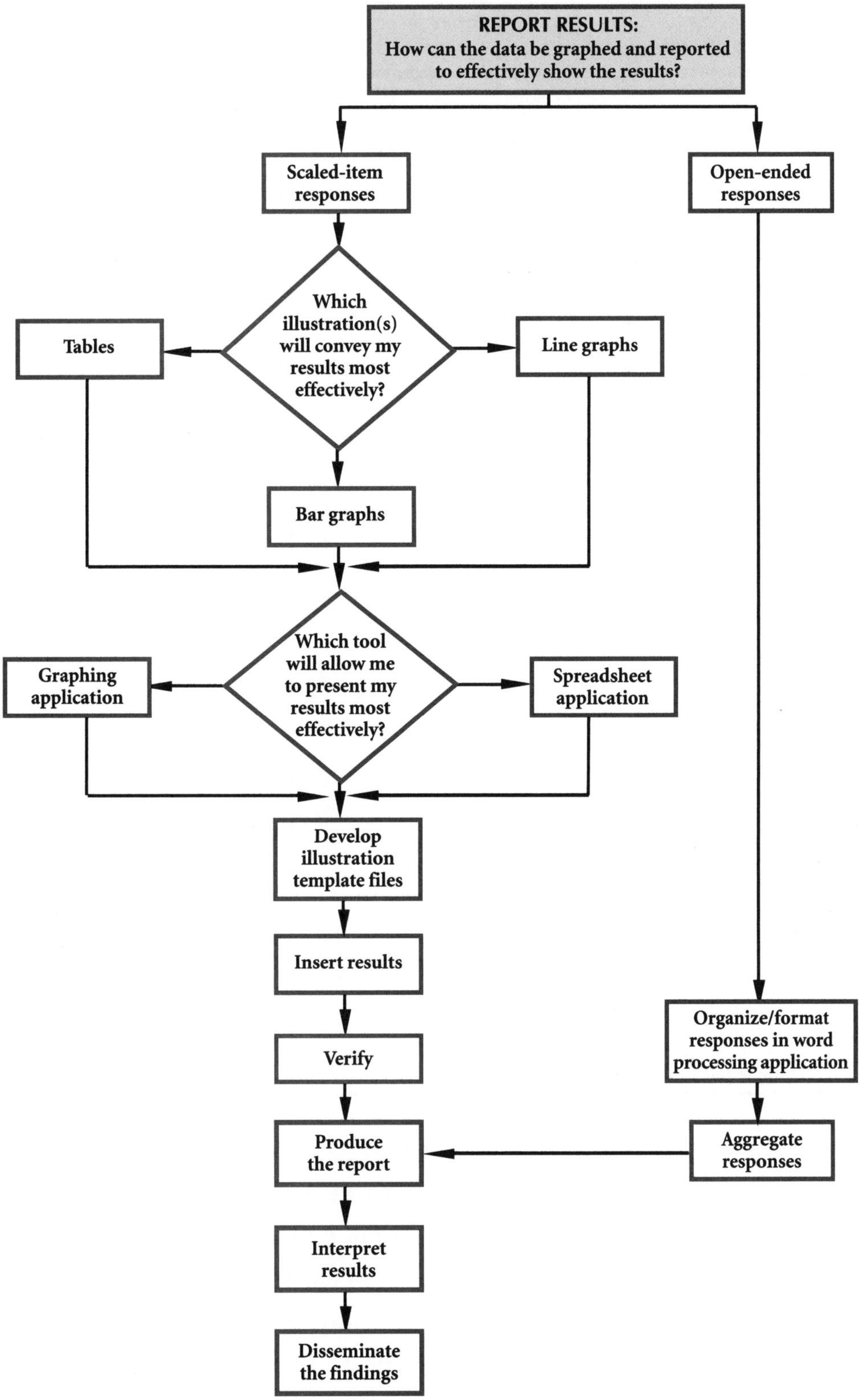

Figure 6.2
QUESTIONNAIRE RESULTS TABLE

ITEM—*When I am at school, I feel:*	Strongly Disagree	Disagree	Neutral	Agree	Strongly Agree
I belong	2%	4%	22%	47%	25%
I am safe	2%	5%	10%	42%	41%
I have fun learning	4%	10%	37%	32%	17%
I like this school	2%	6%	21%	27%	43%
This school is good	1%	4%	21%	38%	37%
I have freedom at school	7%	14%	31%	30%	18%
I have choices in what I learn	9%	20%	42%	22%	8%
My teacher treats me with respect	2%	3%	12%	29%	55%
My teacher cares about me	3%	2%	13%	29%	53%
My teacher thinks I will be successful	2%	3%	14%	36%	44%
My teacher listens to my ideas	2%	3%	26%	44%	25%
My principal cares about me	2%	2%	17%	31%	48%
My teacher is a good teacher	2%	2%	8%	26%	62%
My teacher believes I can learn	1%	1%	10%	29%	59%
I am recognized for good work	3%	5%	29%	41%	22%
I am challenged by the work my teacher asks me to do	8%	8%	42%	25%	17%
The work I do in class makes me think	3%	4%	25%	43%	24%
I know what I am supposed to be learning in my classes	2%	1%	12%	44%	40%
I am a good student	1%	2%	11%	39%	47%
I can be a better student	5%	5%	23%	37%	30%
Quality work is expected at my school	2%	4%	20%	39%	35%
I behave well at school	2%	2%	17%	35%	44%
Students are treated fairly by teachers	7%	7%	19%	28%	38%
Students are treated fairly by the principal	2%	2%	11%	27%	58%
Students are treated fairly by the people on recess duty	10%	13%	22%	30%	24%
Students at my school treat me with respect	8%	7%	38%	30%	18%
Students at my school are friendly	5%	7%	34%	35%	18%
I have lots of friends	3%	4%	18%	31%	44%
I have support for learning at home	2%	3%	15%	35%	44%
My family believes I can do well in school	2%	1%	4%	19%	74%
My family wants me to do well in school	1%	1%	2%	12%	84%

Results could be provided in individual bar graphs that show the percentage of responses for each response option. Figure 6.3 consists of bar graphs for the first four items listed in Figure 6.2. Again, noting the relationship among items becomes very difficult, each item would have a separate bar graph, which results in many pages; and comparing items to each other would require physically comparing each graph to the others to determine any potential relationship. Therefore, it is difficult to determine what actions to take to eliminate undesirable results or to continuously improve desirable results. Alone, individual bar graphs fail to provide a referent point to take action based on the results because the multi-point scale is not summary enough to quickly see the relationship of items to other items. We want to see what we are doing well in relation to what we could be doing better in order to improve.

Figure 6.3
QUESTIONNAIRE RESULTS SHOWN IN BAR GRAPHS

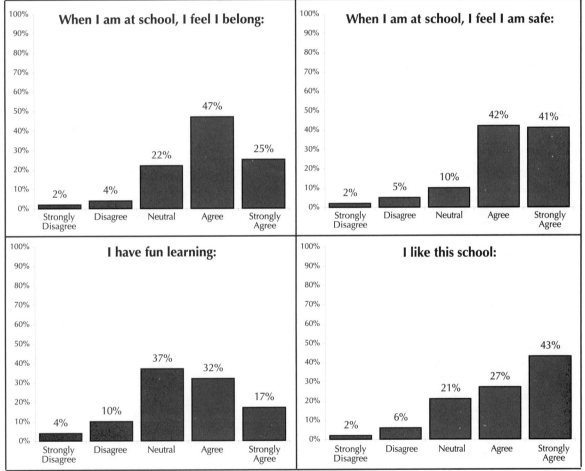

The line graph is a very effective tool for presenting all item responses in relation to each other so that those interpreting the graph have a clear idea of the relationship of the low items to each other, and the high items to each other, and how the lows and the highs are related. Figure 6.4 shows a line graph for the same student questionnaire results shown in Figures 6.2 and 6.3.

Figure 6.4
QUESTIONNAIRE RESULTS SHOWN IN A LINE GRAPH

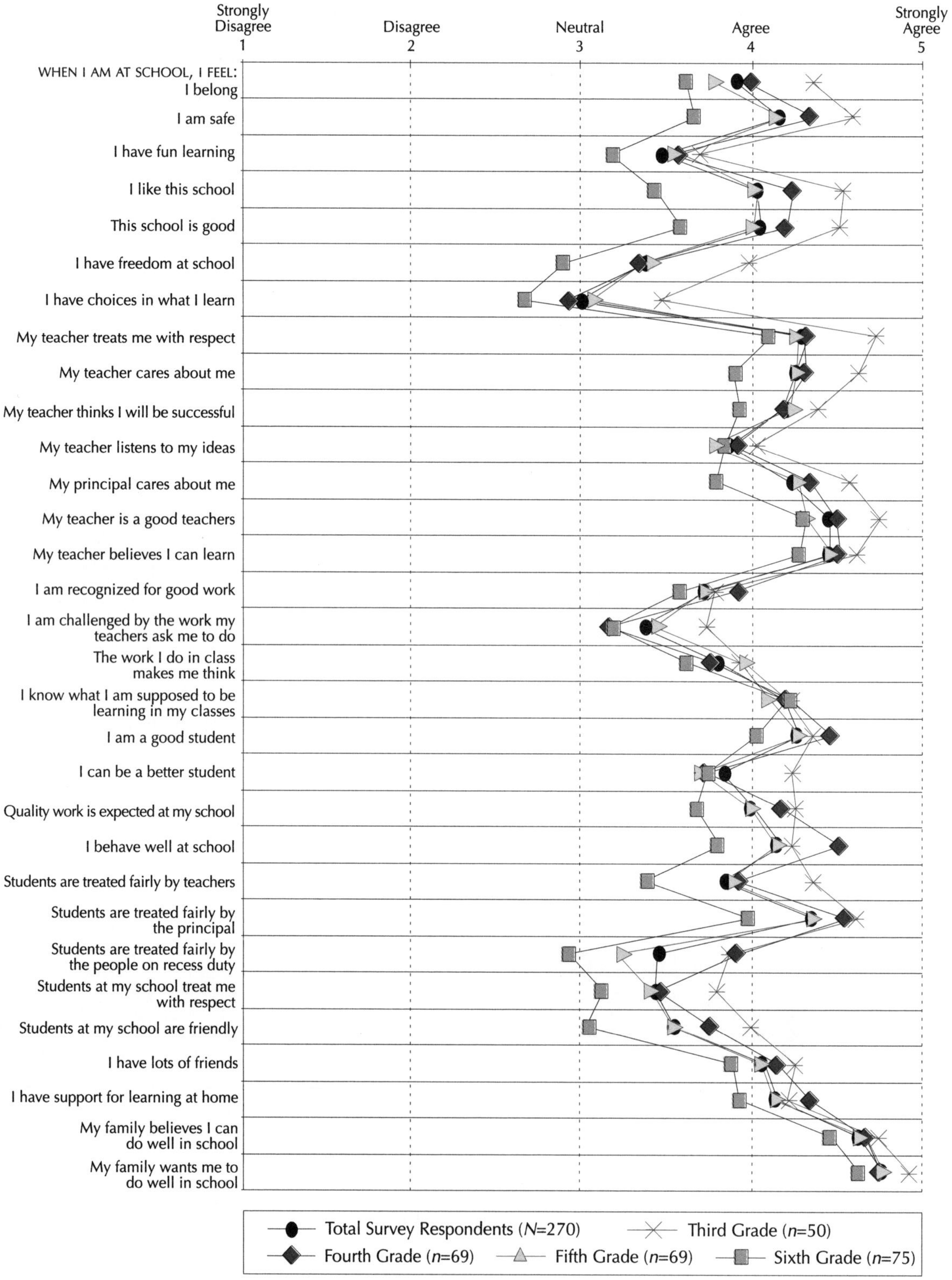

Seeing the relationship of items to each other allows us to leverage what we are doing well and what it might take for us to do better. Also, the disaggregation can quickly show us if there are subgroups with specific issues.

PRESENTATION OF RESULTS

Let's say we have just administered our questionnaire, and we have the raw data ready for analysis. We want to present results that illustrate each item's relationship to all other items. We could produce an average for each item and plot the averages along a line graph so that we can visually present the similarities and differences of the items in relation to each other. The advantages to using a line graph include:

- Simple to produce – this can be done in *Excel* very easily
- Reduce the amount of printed information to a page or two, depending upon the number of questions in the questionnaire
- Present easy-to-read disaggregated results for the demographics asked on the questionnaire
- Results can be distributed and shared easily

Content Driving Presentation

Questionnaire content drives how results are presented. If a variety of scales is used, and if questions employ alternate phrasings, like-items will need to be grouped prior to analysis and presentation of results. Only items that are phrased similarly or scaled similarly should be graphed together. Using a variety of scales may result in additional pages of results, additional graphs for interpretation, and the need for readers to constantly reorient themselves to the scale and presentation being used. Sometimes, using a variety of scales might be a necessary step depending upon the content being administered; but if you can avoid using a variety of scales, you should.

Questionnaire content drives how results are presented.

Tools for Presenting Results

It is tempting to leave the presentation of results to the application being used for analysis. This can be effective if the presentation can be separated from the application for duplication and distribution, but not if the results become proprietary and tied to the analysis application. Tying the use of results to the analysis application means that all those using the results will need to access the application in order to review or share information, limiting access to those with certain technology skills and special training.

Many analysis applications allow the creation of graphs as well as the exporting of files that can be duplicated, shared, and integrated into larger reports without having to be tied to the application itself. The most common output files are formatted as PDF or image files that can be duplicated or printed on their own, easily shared via email or through network drives, and inserted into text documents that describe the findings.

Simple line graphs that illustrate questionnaire items in relation to each other and break-out a variety of subgroups are fairly hard to come by in analysis applications. Each questionnaire would have different questions, a different number of questions, and a variety of subgroups possible. Predicting all of the various combinations to graph proves to be fairly difficult for those trying to automate the building of graphs; therefore, many times display options are not offered.

Spreadsheet applications, with all of their manual capabilities for setting graphing parameters, often offer a wide variety of graphs as well as the ability to customize just about every element within the graph so that a truly professional display of the results can be achieved.

The plus side of using a spreadsheet application for the graphic presentation of results is that many people are familiar with using such applications. The core application is often bundled with most computer purchases, easily accessible without additional cost, and the file sizes are small and very portable. The down side is that we are required to move analyses from one environment to another, crossing yet another data threshold where errors can occur. The creation and use of graphing templates in the spreadsheet application and the automation of moving data from the analysis application to the templates can help reduce the possibility of errors and may be worth the time invested to produce a quality report.

Figure 6.5 shows *Design Considerations for Line Graphs.*

Figure 6.5
DESIGN CONSIDERATIONS FOR LINE GRAPHS

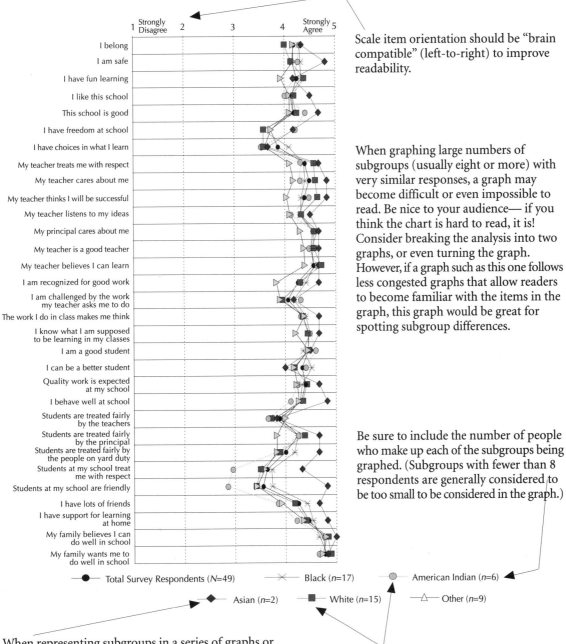

Scale item orientation should be "brain compatible" (left-to-right) to improve readability.

When graphing large numbers of subgroups (usually eight or more) with very similar responses, a graph may become difficult or even impossible to read. Be nice to your audience— if you think the chart is hard to read, it is! Consider breaking the analysis into two graphs, or even turning the graph. However, if a graph such as this one follows less congested graphs that allow readers to become familiar with the items in the graph, this graph would be great for spotting subgroup differences.

Be sure to include the number of people who make up each of the subgroups being graphed. (Subgroups with fewer than 8 respondents are generally considered to be too small to be considered in the graph.)

When representing subgroups in a series of graphs or in graphs from year to year, be consistent with color and with symbols. If Asian students in the school are blue diamonds in one graph, make sure they are presented as blue diamonds in subsequent graphs, so that comparisons can be made easily.

Use symbols that will show up either in color or when the graph is printed or copied in black and white. Each of the subgroups are represented here with different colors and different symbols.

Note: When disaggregating by subgroups, numbers do not always add up to the total number of respondents because some respondents do not identify themselves by the demographic, or they may have the option of indicating more than one subgroup in the demographic.

Presenting Open-Ended Results

While open-ended responses to questions are very time-consuming to aggregate, one can get a complete sense of the learning environment by asking students, for instance, two questions:

◆ *What do you like about this school?*
◆ *What do you wish were different?*

Ask students, staffs, and parents these two questions—

◆ *What are the strengths of this school?*
◆ *What would make the school better?*

Sample student responses:

◆ *What I like most about this school are the teachers. I like the way they have fun making us learn.*
◆ *What I wish were different is, I wish we didn't ever have to leave this school.*

Sample staff and parent responses:

◆ *One of our school's strengths is the good relationship/collaboration among grade-level teachers.*
◆ *Using positive reinforcement in the classroom would make the school better.*

As described in Chapter 5, there are no fast or automated ways to analyze open-ended responses. The best way to analyze open-ended responses is to type the list of open-ended responses (if they were not typed via the online administration route). Review the responses, and add up the number of times students said the same thing. Place the number, in parentheses, after the statement, eliminate the duplicates, and revise your list. You will need to make judgment calls about how to collapse the items when parts of the responses are different.

Figure 6.6 shows a typical final presentation of open-ended results. In presenting open-ended results, some may find it necessary to remove proper names that may single out individuals. There is no rule for removing such information, but it should be considered according to the overall context of the open-ended responses. Proper names can be replaced with indicators such as "my teacher."

Figure 6.6
MIDDLE SCHOOL OPEN-ENDED STAFF RESPONSES

What are the strengths of this school?	*What needs to be improved?*
• Dedicated staff (32) • Extremely talented students (10) • The Arts program (8) • The school's reputation (2) • The teachers' love for their students and their curriculum • Appropriate facilities for our unique program • The parents of the children we teach are wonderful and helpful • Majority of students are motivated to learn • Principal has a strong vision for student achievement • Student diversity	• Incorporate shared decision making so teachers have a voice (12) • An administration that will listen to our input and use our ideas (7) • Time emphasis should be on teachers' teaching (6) • We need more teacher input related to the areas we teach (4) • Teacher morale (3) • Communication among all staff members (3) • Learning-focused teaching strategies (middle school initiative in our district) (2) • Achievement of our impoverished children and slow learners (2) • Learning styles • Literacy instruction for below-grade-level readers

INTERPRET THE RESULTS

The next step is to interpret what the graphs are saying. It is very important to use text that relates to graphs. Additional information to help the audience understand the responses can be added. Figures 6.7 and 6.8 highlight things to look for when interpreting line graphs.

Figure 6.7
TOTAL STUDENT RESPONSES

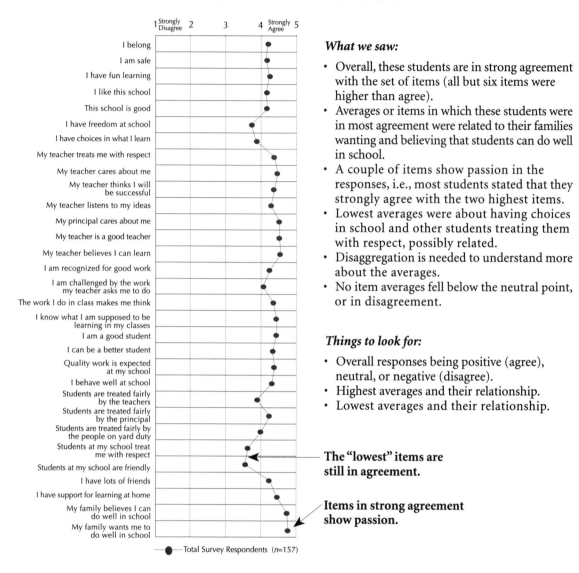

Total Survey Respondents (*n*=157)

What we saw:

- Overall, these students are in strong agreement with the set of items (all but six items were higher than agree).
- Averages or items in which these students were in most agreement were related to their families wanting and believing that students can do well in school.
- A couple of items show passion in the responses, i.e., most students stated that they strongly agree with the two highest items.
- Lowest averages were about having choices in school and other students treating them with respect, possibly related.
- Disaggregation is needed to understand more about the averages.
- No item averages fell below the neutral point, or in disagreement.

Things to look for:

- Overall responses being positive (agree), neutral, or negative (disagree).
- Highest averages and their relationship.
- Lowest averages and their relationship.

The "lowest" items are still in agreement.

Items in strong agreement show passion.

Figure 6.8 shows the same questionnaire responses broken down by grade level. The figure highlights various points of interest to consider and some recommendations for further problem analysis.

Figure 6.8
STUDENT RESPONSES COMPARED BY GRADE LEVEL

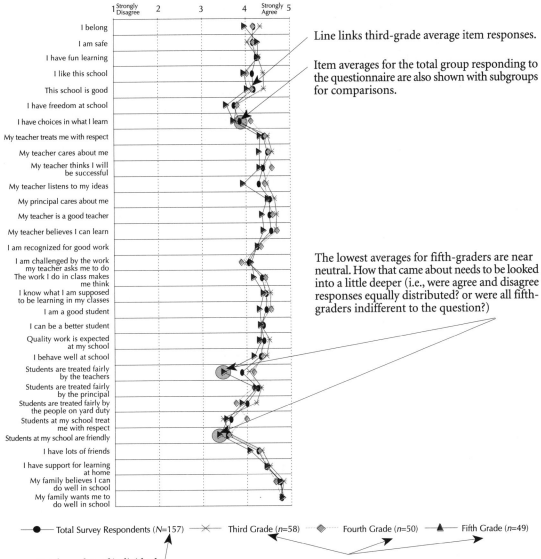

Line links third-grade average item responses.

Item averages for the total group responding to the questionnaire are also shown with subgroups for comparisons.

The lowest averages for fifth-graders are near neutral. How that came about needs to be looked into a little deeper (i.e., were agree and disagree responses equally distributed? or were all fifth-graders indifferent to the question?)

● Total Survey Respondents (*N*=157) ✕ Third Grade (*n*=58) ◆ Fourth Grade (*n*=50) ▲ Fifth Grade (*n*=49)

Total number of individuals responding to the questionnaire.

Subgroups that make-up the total. In this case, it is grade level. (Subgroups fewer than 8 are generally considered to be too small to be considered in the graph.)

Things to look for:

- Subgroups that "stick out" or look different from the others.
- Big gaps among one subgroup and the other subgroups.
- Differences in averages that result in opposite responses, such as agree-disagree.
- Subgroup trends that are unexpected.
- Size of subgroup that looks different from the other groups, although small numbers may indicate items that still need to be addressed.
- Other analyses that would provide further understandings of the responses.

What we saw:

- There are few real differences among group averages.
- Third graders tend to be in strongest agreement with items on the questionnaire.
- Fifth graders tend to be in least agreement with questionnaire items.
- Fourth grade responses consistently fall in the middle of all the subgroups.
- Staff might want to understand how averages came about (i.e., look at the distribution of responses.)

PRODUCE THE REPORT

Documenting the findings and listing the next steps that come from the analyses are crucial. This documentation keeps groups from repeating what they have already done, provides them with information related to where they are right now, and jump-starts their thinking on next steps.

A complete report describes all items and their relationship to each other and to the overall questionnaire purpose. Figure 6.9 shows an example report.

Along with questionnaire results, the following should be included:

- Why the questionnaire was administered
- The setting in which it was administered
- Unique features of the questionnaire
- Type of questionnaire
- Number of respondents (total and sample populations)
- Response rate
- How long the questionnaire project took to complete
- General content of questionnaire
- Analysis and graphs
- Interpretation of results
- Recommendations/next steps

Figure 6.9
INTERPRETING LINE GRAPHS—SAMPLE NARRATIVE ANALYSIS

Students in grade three through five at Archer Elementary School responded to an *Education for the Future* questionnaire designed to measure how they feel about their learning environment. Students were asked to respond to items using a five-point scale: 1=strongly disagree; 2=disagree; 3=neutral; 4=agree; and, 5=strongly agree.

Average responses to each item on the questionnaire were graphed by the totals. The icons in the graph show the average responses to each item. The line joins the icons to help the reader know the distribution results. The line has no other meaning.

Total Student Responses

Figure 6.9
INTERPRETING LINE GRAPHS—SAMPLE NARRATIVE ANALYSIS

Students were most passionate in their responses (scoring between 4.5 and 4.8 on the five-point scale), to the following items, in descending order:

- My family wants me to do well in school
- My family believes I can do well in school
- My family believes I can learn
- My principal cares about me
- My teacher is a good teacher

Students were in next strongest agreement (falling above 4.25 on the scale) with the following items, in descending order:

- My teacher cares about me
- I know what I am supposed to be learning in my classes
- I am a good student
- I have support for learning at home
- My teacher treats me with respect
- Quality work is expected at my school
- My teacher thinks I will be successful
- The work I do in class makes me think
- I can be a better student
- I behave well at school
- My teacher listens to my ideas

The items which elicited a positive response that fell above 4.0 on the scale were, in descending order:

- I am recognized for good work
- Students are treated fairly by the principal
- I have lots of friends
- I have fun learning
- I belong
- This school is good
- I am safe
- I like this school
- I am challenged by the work my teacher asks me to do

Followed closely by, and continuing in agreement (above 3.5 on the scale), with the statements, in descending order:

- Students are treated fairly by the people on yard duty
- Students are treated fairly by teachers
- I have choices in what I learn
- I have freedom at school
- Students at my school treat me with respect
- Students at my school are friendly

Disseminate the Findings

Once the report is written, you will need to determine the best way in which to get a summary of the analyzed results to the respondents and other interested parties. You may need to meet in person with target groups to share what was learned and to discuss next steps together. Think about what was promised when the questionnaire was administered—follow through on your word.

Just as important as getting the questionnaire constructed and appropriately analyzed is the use of the questionnaire results. It is important never to use one piece of data in isolation from the numerous other pieces of data available to schools. It is also important, whenever in doubt of what the results say, to ask respondent groups to clarify meaning through follow-up interviews or focus groups.

Whether the meaning of the results is analyzed by a small group or by the entire staff, the results must be shared with all school personnel as quickly as possible so next steps can be formulated and agreed upon. Chapter 7 discusses how to share and use questionnaire results with staffs.

Just as important as getting the questionnaire constructed and appropriately analyzed is the use of the questionnaire results.

READER CHALLENGE

What applications, currently licensed by your school district, can help you present your results most effectively?

Can you breathe new life into results from previously administered questionnaires by presenting them in line graphs?

Can you breathe new life into results from previously administered questionnaires by presenting the open-ended responses more effectively?

SUMMARY

Graphs and charts make the results of questionnaires easy to understand for school personnel, parents, and the community. Whenever possible, the results should be presented in easily understandable ways to enable the audience to analyze the findings and to determine what next steps are necessary to change undesirable results.

CHAPTER **7**

USING QUESTIONNAIRE RESULTS

This chapter explains how to get
questionnaire results shared and used.

So, what do we do with all the pretty graphs we made from our questionnaire administration and analysis? Because the results of our questionnaire data analysis are about the school as a whole, and because it is the staffs that have to do something about the results, the graphs need to go to the staffs for review and analysis. The more we get the staffs working with the results, the more they will own and use them to improve teaching and learning throughout the school. There may not be one ideal way to share questionnaire results and graphs with all staff members, but several approaches have been effective.

> *The more we get the staffs working with the results, the more they will own and use them to improve teaching and learning throughout the school.*

DETERMINE PURPOSE:
What do you want to learn? How do you want to use the results in conjunction with your school improvement plan?

DETERMINE CONTENT:
What content is desired and from whom?

DEVELOP INSTRUMENT AND PILOT:
Create instrument, pilot, and revise as necessary. Is the questionnaire working the way you want it to work?

COLLECT THE DATA:
How will the questionnaire be administered and when?

ANALYZE RESULTS:
How can the results be analyzed to show the information gleaned from the questionnaire?

REPORT RESULTS:
How can the data be graphed and reported to effectively show the results?

SHARE AND REVIEW RESULTS:
How and when are you going to share results with stakeholders?

SHARING WITH STAFF

To be used, the results must be shared personally with staffs. Figure 7.1 breaks down the steps in sharing/reviewing results. Nothing can undermine the staffs' acceptance of data results quicker than reading or hearing about them before the results have been shared with all the staff. There are several ways to share and review questionnaire results with staffs. These approaches can be done with just the questionnaire results or with all the data in a data profile. All approaches start with each faculty member having her/his own copy of the questionnaire results. Some effective approaches include the following, which are briefly described below. You and your staff will need to determine which approaches will work the best.

- Committee review meetings
- Fish bowl
- Gallery walk
- Small groups with protocol
- Data party
- Review as a part of overall data profile
- Forcefield analysis

Figure 7.1
SHARE AND REVIEW RESULTS WITH STAFFS

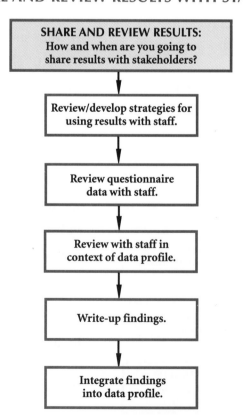

Committee Review Meetings

Individual faculty members could serve on committees assigned to review the student, staff, or parent results. The committees' charges would be to thoroughly review the results of the questionnaire to look for the strengths, challenges, and implications for the continuous improvement plan. Each committee would report its findings to the entire staff. Staff members not on a specific committee could add what they saw. Implications across the three questionnaires will be melded into one set of overall implications/recommendations for improvement.

Fish Bowl

Fishbowls are used for dynamic group involvement. The most common configuration is an "inner ring," consisting of four to five chairs arranged in an inner circle, which is the discussion group, surrounded by a concentric circle "outer rings," which is the observation group. Just as people observe the fish in the fishbowl, the outer rings observe the inner ring. The people in the inner ring (volunteers) discuss what they see in a graph (five minutes each), while the outer rings listen. The individuals in the outer rings are not allowed to speak until they join the inner circle. When an individual in the inner ring is finished speaking or finished with her/his observations, she/he moves to the empty outer ring chair, and someone from the outer ring wanting to say something moves to the empty chair in the inner ring. A questionnaire could be reviewed and discussed in 30 minutes. The facilitator could make variations to the rules to get input from all observers.

Gallery Walk

With the questionnaire graphs grouped by respondent and posted on the wall, along with sheets of chart paper with *strengths, challenges,* and *implications* for the continuous improvement plan written on them, a gallery walk gives staff members an opportunity to look over the data—independently and interdependently—and to write the first things that come to mind when they see the graphs. A facilitator directs staff members to form groups and take turns looking at the student, staff, and parent graphs. The facilitator leads the discussions of findings.

Small Faculty Groups with Protocol

Each faculty member could be assigned to a small group of five to seven (with grade level and subject area mixings) to review either the student, staff, or parent questionnaire results. With a protocol for reviewing the results, the conversation can be fun and respectful. A protocol could be something like this: One person speaks for three minutes about what she/he sees in a graph, without questions. Another person takes three minutes to add what she/he observed, and so forth, until the questionnaire has been analyzed. The group is given 15 minutes to discuss what it wants to report to the entire faculty. A recorder documents and reports the highlights to other small groups reviewing the same questionnaire. In 10 minutes they merge their findings and present to the entire staff.

Data Party

All the disaggregated and total graphs of the student, staff, and parent questionnaires results can be handed out to staff members who would review a graph for highlights and then seek out another disaggregated graph from the other respondents and compare notes. For example, if I got the student graph disaggregated by ethnicity, I would review that data and then seek out the parent questionnaire disaggregated by ethnicity. (There probably will not be a staff questionnaire disaggregated by ethnicity, as the subgroups would be too small.) A facilitator could provide a posted list of different graphs to compare, or use stickers, or draw names to get the faculty talking to each other about the results. This activity could be accompanied with refreshments if staffs would not feel that this trivializes the importance of sharing the data results.

Review as a Part of the Data Profile

If the timing is right, all data can be a part of the processes described above. The difference is that the implications for demographics, student learning, school processes, and perceptions can then be merged to find the big elements or concepts that must be a part of the continuous improvement plan (See *Questions to Guide the Study of Questionnaire Results,* Figure 7.2, on the opposite page).

Figure 7.2
QUESTIONS TO GUIDE THE STUDY OF QUESTIONNAIRE RESULTS

1. What are your perceptual *strengths* and *challenges*?	
Strengths	*Challenges*

2. What are some *implications* for your school improvement plan?

3. Looking at the data presented, what other perceptual data would you want to answer the question *How do we do business?* for your school?

Besides looking at the strengths, challenges, and implications for the continuous improvement plan, staffs might choose to use a questionnaire table such as the one shown in Figure 7.3, on the following page, to analyze the results across the different respondents.

Figure 7.3
ANALYSIS OF QUESTIONNAIRE DATA

	Student Questionnaire	Staff Questionnaire	Parent Questionnaire	Agreements Across Questionnaires	Disagreements Across Questionnaires
General Feel of Questionnaire *(positive, neutral, negative)*					
Most Positive Items					
Neutral Items					
Negative Items					
On which items are there differences in subgroups? *(i.e., disaggregated responses)*					
Comments					

Forcefield Analysis

A *forcefield analysis* could also be used to display the driving forces, the results that move the school toward change, and the restraining forces—the results keeping the school from getting to where it wants to be. A forcefield analysis is displayed below in Figure 7.4. Starting with a school goal, or "ideal state," a forcefield analysis requires teams to look at questionnaire results for driving forces and restraining forces. This could be used with data only, or with brainstormed ideas, as well.

Figure 7.4
IDEAL STATE—ALL STUDENTS READING
AT GRADE LEVEL BY GRADE THREE

Driving Forces	Restraining Forces
Fits with priorities	Our research does not support this possibility
What teachers want for kids	Class sizes are too large
Fits with the purpose of the school	Not enough money to incorporate the programs that are necessary
School board desires	No systematic measurements to know how we are doing
Reading Recovery can help	Reading specialist is needed
Parents do not like the way students are being taught	Families do not help with homework
We need better processes for teaching reading	Students are not native English speakers
Students like to go to school here	No agreement on what constitutes reading at grade level
Teachers want to improve	Kids are living in poverty
We need strong measurements	Students do not behave
Teachers need to create a continuum of learning that makes sense for students	Time
	No money for professional development
	No measurement of where students are with respect to reading at grades K, 1, 2, 3

Once the results have been shared and reviewed with the staff, how they will be used to improve teaching and learning should be part of the agenda for each department meeting and schoolwide staff meeting. The results should drive the professional learning of the staff and the continuous improvement plan.

The Write-Up

The Leadership Team or Action Team is typically responsible for writing the analysis of the questionnaire results for the data profile and sharing it with staffs and the community. Staff members should always be the first group to review the questionnaire results and the write-up. After the results have been shared with staffs and students, the highlights can be shared with respondents and the community at a public Board of Education meeting and with the media.

Integrating the Results into the School Profile

The final step in documenting results is integrating them into the overall school profile, which provides a context for questionnaire results along with demographic, student learning, and school process data. Each type of data will have what staffs see as strengths, challenges, and implications for the continuous improvement plan. Strengths, challenges, and implications for the continuous improvement plan across the four types of data will be merged and documented to be included in the continuous improvement plan. For more information, please see the following books, all published by *Eye on Education:*

- *Data, Data Everywhere* (2009).

- *Translating Data into Information to Improve Teaching and Learning* (2007).

- A four-book (with CD-Roms) collection of *Using Data to Improve Student Learning—in Elementary Schools* (2003); *in Middle Schools* (2004); *in High Schools* (2005); and *in School Districts* (2006).

- *Data Analysis for Continuous School Improvement* (First Edition, 1998; Second Edition, 2004).

- *The School Portfolio Toolkit: A Planning, Implementation, and Evaluation Guide for Continuous School Improvement,* with CD-Rom (2002).

- *The Example School Portfolio* (2000).

- *The School Portfolio: A Comprehensive Framework for School Improvement* (First Edition, 1994; Second Edition, 1999).

USING THE RESULTS

When using questionnaire results to drive continuous school improvement, staff members often want to tackle the most negative item or items first, and sometimes, only. It is important to understand the big picture that the results are showing, and to understand the true meaning behind the responses, so that the results can be dealt with efficiently and effectively.

Consider the relationship of the items to each other. Let's say we have five low items. If we take the items literally and separately, we would be looking at five different things to do, which we probably will not get to, when in actuality, the five are most probably related, and a serious consequence to making progress.

Consider, for example, the Staff Questionnaire. Often *staff morale* is the lowest response item for teachers. Some schools making a knee jerk reaction have started adding snacks in the teachers' lounges and a once a month social to improve morale. Schools that look at the morale in context to the other items are doing something else. They will see that the other low item responses are about having a clear and shared vision, strong collaboration, leadership to help all teachers implement the vision, and professional learning to help all teachers implement the vision. Looking at the items together, it appears that revisiting the vision would be a great place to start. While revisiting the vision, staffs can detail the type of leadership and professional learning that is needed to implement the vision, and what it will take for everyone to understand and implement with vision.

With respect to the Student Questionnaire: Let's say the lowest item is *students treating each other with respect*. We need to look at all the other low items, as well as what the students tell us in the open-ended items to understand what they are trying to tell us, and what else is behind the responses. Sometimes the adults are not treating the students with respect. Therefore, the logical next step is to revisit the way all adults and children are treating each other, and design strategies to improve respect for all.

In short, to really use the items, staffs have to understand the big picture, and determine solutions that can effectively work across the items.

READER CHALLENGE

How will you share your results with stakeholders?

SUMMARY

Reviewing the results of student, staff, and parent questionnaires can and should be fun. Use whatever creative approaches that might work with your staff and others with whom you will be sharing questionnaire results. After the data are shared and reviewed, action items must be determined from the results, in relationship to the other school data, such as demographics, student learning, and school process data. Then something must be done to use the data to improve. Use the data to support the implementation of the vision and the learning environment.

CHAPTER **8**

INTEGRATING QUESTIONNAIRE FINDINGS INTO COMPREHENSIVE DATA ANALYSIS: AN EXAMPLE

This chapter shows how perceptual data helped Table Mountain Middle School improve its operations for all students.

Table Mountain Middle School enjoyed a long history of getting good results—that is until *No Child Left Behind* (NCLB) came around. When NCLB required student achievement results to be disaggregated, staff members found there was quite a discrepancy among the scores Caucasian students were receiving and the scores the small populations of African-American and Hispanic students were receiving on their state proficiency exams.

Overall, approximately 80% of the Table Mountain students were proficient on both the English/Language Arts and Mathematics tests. Disaggregated, African-American and Hispanic students scored 40% and 50% proficient, respectively.

After receiving these results, the first reaction of the school personnel was to set up interventions—mostly after school and tutoring programs—for the 20% of students who did not achieve proficiency. Some students were encouraged to arrive at school at 6:00 a.m. for extra help and/or to remain after school until 6:00 p.m. to complete homework. Teachers were hoping the additional programs would get the students to meet the teachers' instructional expectations. Even though the students were not expected to follow the instruction during class time, they were expected to sit all day in the regular classes and to catch up before or after regular school hours.

At the end of the year, the state assessments showed essentially no gains for the "remediated" students. Some scores even decreased.

Not wanting similar results at the end of the next year, staff members determined it was time to hear from the students, teachers, and parents about what they thought would improve student achievement results.

Table Mountain Middle School students, staffs, and parents completed *Education for the Future* questionnaires. Students and staffs also answered two open-ended questions. The results follow.

STUDENT QUESTIONNAIRE RESULTS

Ninety-five percent of the students in grades six through eight at Table Mountain Middle School responded to the *Education for the Future* questionnaire designed to measure how they feel about their learning environment. Students were asked to respond to items using a five-point scale: 1=strongly disagree; 2=disagree; 3=neutral; 4=agree; and, 5=strongly agree. Average responses to each item on the questionnaire were graphed and disaggregated by gender, grade level, and ethnicity. Some of the graphs are shown on the pages that follow along with a summary of results. (*Note:* The icons in the graphs show the average responses to each item by the disaggregation indicated in the legend. The lines join the icons to help the reader know the distribution results for each disaggregation. The lines have no other meaning. *Also note:* Some of the subgroup numbers do not add up to the total number of respondents because some respondents did not identify themselves by the demographic or identified themselves by more than one demographic.)

Figure 8.1 shows average student responses to all the items in the student questionnaire in addition to the responses disaggregated by grade level. The overall results were in agreement, with the exception of five items that were neutral. These items were: *I have freedom at school; I have choices in what I learn;* and *Students are treated fairly by teachers.* The graph revealed some slight differences when disaggregated by grade level. Sixth graders' results were generally the highest in agreement, while eighth graders were generally in lowest agreement.

Student questionnaire data were also disaggregated by ethnicity (414 White; 122 Black; 97 Other; 46 Asian; and 34 Hispanic/Latino students responded). Responses revealed some differences (Figure 8.2). Asian students generally responded less positively than other subgroups.

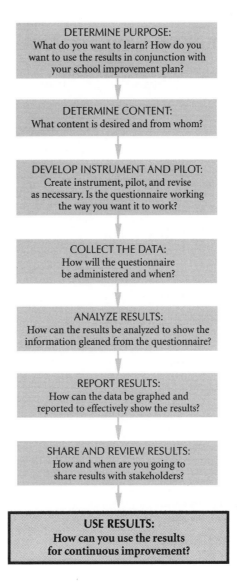

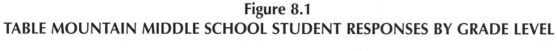

Figure 8.1
TABLE MOUNTAIN MIDDLE SCHOOL STUDENT RESPONSES BY GRADE LEVEL

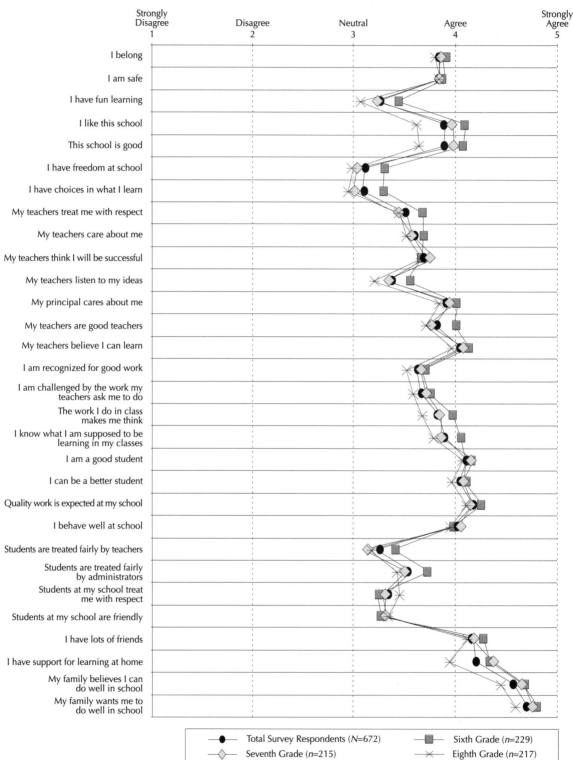

Figure 8.2
TABLE MOUNTAIN MIDDLE SCHOOL STUDENT RESPONSES BY ETHNICITY

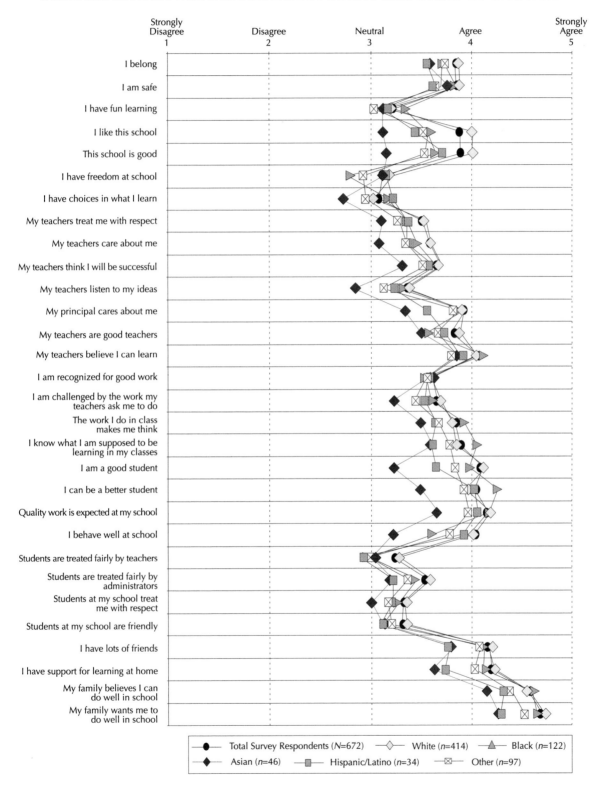

Student Open-Ended Responses

Table Mountain Middle School students were asked to respond to two open-ended questions: *What do you like about your school?* and *What do you wish was different at your school?* The top ten responses are shown below.

1. *What do you like about your school?*

   ♦ Good teachers (145)

   ♦ This school has a very strong arts program (98)

   ♦ My friends (51)

   ♦ The class choices we have for electives (30)

   ♦ Gym (27)

   ♦ Nothing (23)

   ♦ Learning can be fun (14)

   ♦ The people (14)

   ♦ The band program (10)

   ♦ My work is challenging (9)

2. *What do you wish was different at your school?*

   ♦ Less strict dress code (65)

   ♦ Teachers more respectful of all students (59)

   ♦ Better lunches and more food in the cafeteria (53)

   ♦ Bigger hallways (37)

   ♦ Cleaner bathrooms with locks on the doors (32)

   ♦ Less homework and fewer projects (25)

   ♦ Students would treat each other better (20)

   ♦ No teaming (14)

   ♦ Be able to chew gum (8)

   ♦ More freedom (7)

PARENT QUESTIONNAIRE RESULTS

Three-hundred fifty parents (75% response rate) of students attending Table Mountain Middle School completed an online questionnaire during spring parent-teacher conferences. The questionnaire was designed to measure their perceptions of the school environment. Parents were asked to respond to items using a five-point scale: 1=strongly disagree; 2=disagree; 3=neutral; 4=agree; and, 5=strongly agree.

Average responses to each item on the questionnaire were graphed and disaggregated by ethnicity, children's grade levels, number of children in the household, and number of children in the school.

Average Parent Responses

In general, the average responses to the parent questionnaire indicated agreement to the items listed. The item averages are shown on the graphs that follow in Figures 8.3 through 8.5.

Parent Responses by Ethnicity

Parent questionnaire data were disaggregated by ethnicity: 274 White; 32 Black; 18 Hispanic/Latino; 17 Asian; and 16 Other (Figure 8.3). Results show that Black and Other parents were generally less positive in their responses. Some differences were noted, although most averages were in agreement. The lowest averages were neutral. Once again, we must take the small Ns into consideration.

Figure 8.3
TABLE MOUNTAIN MIDDLE SCHOOL PARENT RESPONSES BY ETHNICITY

Parent Responses by Children's Grade Levels

Parent questionnaire responses disaggregated by children's grade levels revealed few differences. No significant distinguishing pattern emerged when looking at the data by these subgroups. (Graph not shown here.)

Parent Responses by Number of Children in the School

Parent questionnaire data disaggregated by the number of children in the school clustered around the overall average and revealed few differences in responses. (Graph not shown here.)

Parent Responses by Number of Children in the Household

Parent questionnaire data were also disaggregated by the number of children in the household (one child, $n=62$; two children, $n=158$; three children, $n=82$; and four children, $n=24$). Results graphed by this demographic revealed slight differences in responses. Parents with four children responded lower to the items in the questionnaire than did the parents with one, two, or three children (see Figure 8.4).

Figure 8.4
TABLE MOUNTAIN MIDDLE SCHOOL PARENT RESPONSES
BY NUMBER OF CHILDREN IN THE HOUSEHOLD

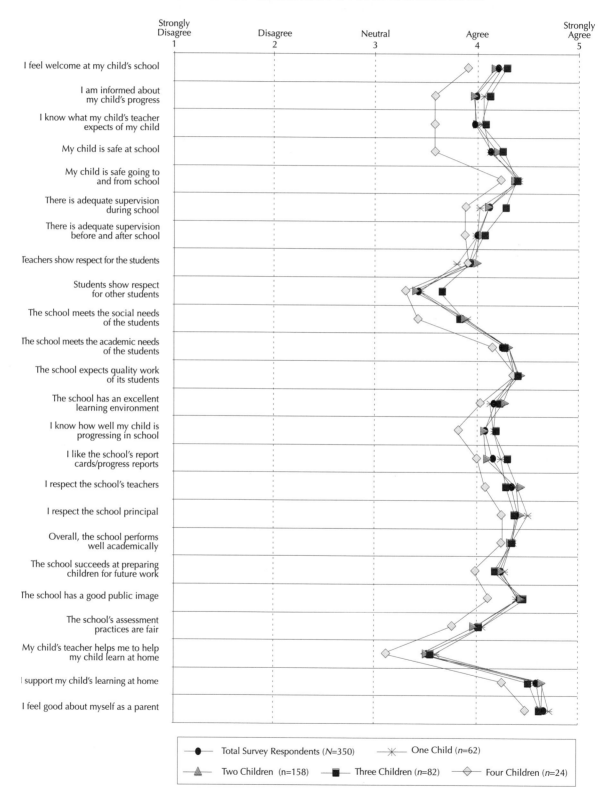

STAFF QUESTIONNAIRE RESULTS

Table Mountain staff members (n=49, 98% response rate) responded to a questionnaire designed to measure their perceptions of the school environment. Members of the staff were asked to respond to items using a five-point scale: 1=strongly disagree; 2=disagree; 3=neutral; 4=agree; and 5=strongly agree.

Average responses to the items on the questionnaire were graphed and disaggregated by number of years teaching. The results were not disaggregated by gender and ethnicity because the resulting male subgroup was so small that individuals could be identified.

Average Staff Responses

Overall, the average responses to the staff questionnaire indicated agreement with most of the items in the questionnaire. The average for the total group is graphed in Figure 8.5 (two-page graph) with the results disaggregated by number of years of teaching. Results graphed by the number of years of teaching (one to three years, n=5; four to six years, n=5; seven to ten years, n=8; and eleven or more years, n=31) revealed some apparent differences in responses. The most apparent difference is that teachers with one to three years of teaching responded lowest on most items. Although, the first three subgroups are very small, they are displayed at this time for discussion purposes.

Figure 8.5
TABLE MOUNTAIN MIDDLE SCHOOL STAFF RESPONSES
BY NUMBER OF YEARS TEACHING

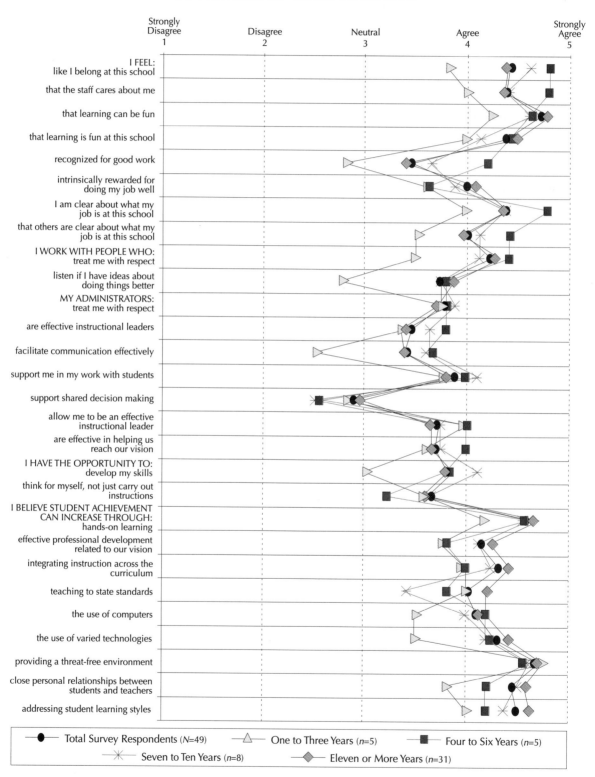

Figure 8.5 *(Continued)*
TABLE MOUNTAIN MIDDLE SCHOOL STAFF RESPONSES
BY NUMBER OF YEARS TEACHING

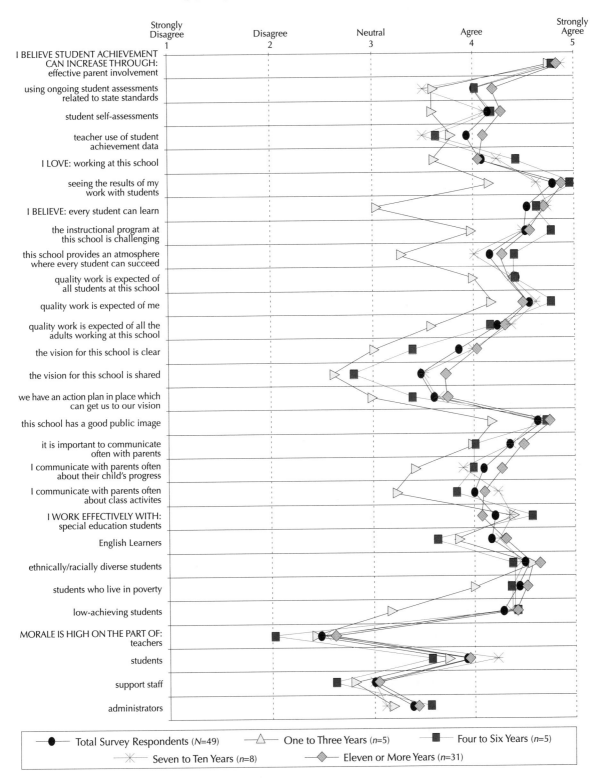

Staff Open-Ended Responses

Table Mountain Middle School staff responded to two open-ended questions in May 2008: *What are the strengths of this school?* and *What needs to be improved?* The top results are shown below.

1. *What are the strengths of this school?*

   ◆ Dedicated staff (32)

   ◆ Extremely talented students (10)

   ◆ The Arts program (8)

   ◆ The school's reputation (2)

   ◆ The teachers' love for their students and their curriculum (2)

   ◆ Appropriate facilities for our unique program (2)

   ◆ The parents of the children we teach are wonderful and helpful (2)

2. *What needs to be improved?*

   ◆ Incorporate shared decision making so teachers have a voice (11)

   ◆ Teacher morale (3)

   ◆ Communication among all staff members (3)

   ◆ Standards-based instruction with higher-order assessments (2)

   ◆ Teacher leadership (2)

Standards Assessment

Thirty-six teachers (72% response rate) at Table Mountain Middle School responded to an *Education for the Future Standards Assessment Questionnaire* for middle school teachers. The questionnaire contained nine questions, asking how well teachers know the state/district content standards, and to what degree they are implementing the standards. A summary of the results for questions one through four is shown in Figure 8.6 in two different ways—(a) Average responses in a line graph, followed by (b) Percentage responding to each response option shown in a bar graph.

Figure 8.6
TABLE MOUNTAIN MIDDLE SCHOOL STAFF RESPONSES

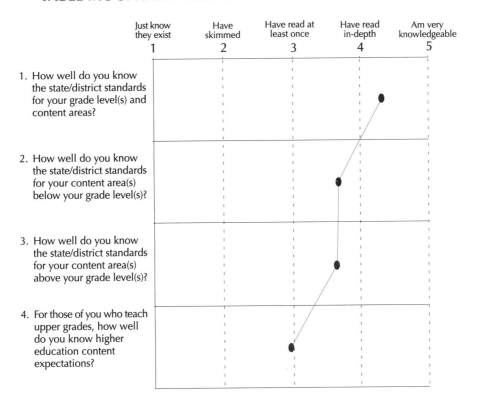

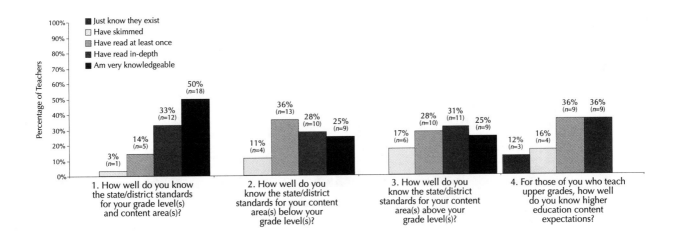

Figure 8.6 *(Continued)*
TABLE MOUNTAIN MIDDLE SCHOOL STAFF RESPONSES

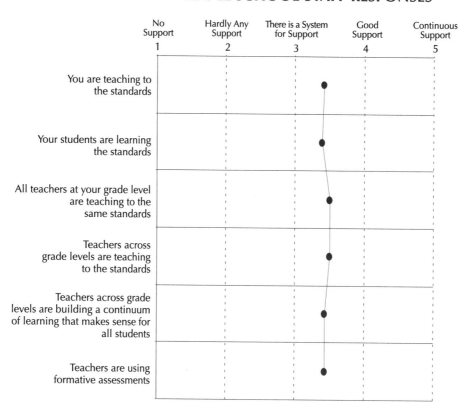

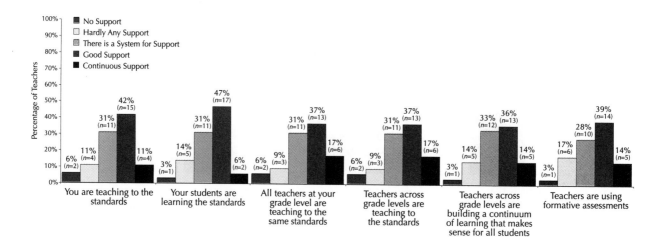

In addition to the above statements, teachers added comments about other things that would help them better know the standards:

- We need more time to teach and plan—we don't have the time to get to all of the standards. (3)

- The instructional coaching that we are getting now does not affect all areas of instruction.

- Planning with other teachers in the district that teach my subject and grade level, with continued contact as the year progresses.

- Quality peer coaching.

- Professional learning sessions especially for my content area—not generic sessions that cross all, or multiple disciplines (i.e., not Fine Arts, but a session for Visual Arts, Dance).

In addition to the above statements, teachers added comments about what they would like their learning organization to do to help them ensure that all students are meeting the state/district content standards:

- We need specific content area meeting time with other schools/teachers in the same area. (6)

- Smaller classes. (3)

- We need to get parents of reluctant learners more involved.

- Less quantity, more quality.

- I felt lost not being prepared for the new and totally different Language Arts standards.

ANALYZING THE RESULTS FOR POSITIVE CHANGE

Using the questionnaire results with their other data (i.e., demographics, student learning, and school processes), staff members determined the following:

- Staff might need to re-think discipline policies/strategies, how everyone respects each other, and the dress code.

- Even though most parents are generally satisfied with the school, there is less parental agreement with the idea that students and teachers show mutual respect.

- Not all parents feel teachers help them to help their children learn at home.

- Staff needs to revisit the vision to bring newer teachers on board.

- Staff might need to work with parents to help them help their children learn at home.

- Staff needs to implement strategies to improve communication, collaboration, and morale.

- Staff needs to develop strategies to get all teachers knowing and implementing strategies.

After discussing and agreeing on these items, staff members determined that they should focus their professional learning on revisiting the vision for their school, developing strategies to improve communication (among staff members and with parents) and increasing collaboration (within and among grade levels and departments). They also agreed to create a Professional Learning Community to help all of them teach to the standards.

READER CHALLENGE

*Do you know how you will use your questionnaire results
with all your data to continuously improve?*

SUMMARY

Perceptions data can help school personnel see the school from the perspective of students, parents, and staffs.

Perceptions data can help school personnel see the school from the perspective of students, parents, and staffs. These data can bring insight to student achievement results and provide all personnel with information for improvement that they would not see otherwise.

Developing a plan that considers perceptual data, along with demographic, student learning, and school process data, helps ensure that multiple measures of data are included and progress in all these areas will be monitored and evaluated.

CHAPTER 9

EDUCATION FOR THE FUTURE QUESTIONNAIRES: FROM DEVELOPMENT TO USE

This chapter describes how the Education for the Future questionnaires were developed and how they are used.

In 1991, while working intensively with a group of schools that were looking for ways to improve their results, *Education for the Future* created questionnaires to help the schools understand their learning environments from the perspective of students, staffs, administrators, and parents. The schools thought they were doing a good job, but they did not have any real input from their customers and staff members. The casual conversations in the school halls and teachers' lounge, at extracurricular events, parent conferences, and the grocery store provided narrow observations; and the schools wanted to hear from a wider range of those who lived in the community and those who were directly impacted by the services that the schools offered. *Education for the Future* designed, administered, analyzed, and presented the results of the questionnaires. The questionnaire results helped each of the schools improve its procedures and operations and get student achievement increases.

Today, *Education for the Future* continues to use updated versions of these questionnaires—across the United States as well as in other countries.

Education for the Future has added related questionnaires to its collection, currently offering more than a dozen different questionnaires to assist schools and districts with continuous improvement. (The questionnaires are available for download on the *Education for the Future* website: *http://eff.csuchico.edu.*)

This chapter describes how these questionnaires were developed and how they are used today. Definitions of validity and reliability are presented first.

VALIDITY

Validity is about asking the right questions to justify what you get in the end. If the content of a questionnaire matches a situation that is being studied, then the questionnaire has content validity.

> *Validity is about asking the right questions to justify what you get in the end.*

The content of the *Education for the Future* questionnaires was validated during the process of questionnaire development. Items were drafted based on the literature about effective schools and included issues important to students and teachers interviewed by *Education for the Future* staff before, during, and after questionnaire administration. The questionnaires were revised after years of input from all parties and are updated regularly. The reasons we use the items or questions we use (shown in Figures 9.1 through 9.3 on pages 134-138) are discussed later in this chapter.

RELIABILITY

Reliability is a measure of an assessment instrument, such as a questionnaire, that says that if we give the same instrument over time, we will get the same or similar results.

> *Reliability is a measure of an assessment instrument, such as a questionnaire, that says that if we give the same instrument over time, we will get the same or similar results.*

Education for the Future wanted its questionnaires to be reliable. However, we also wanted the questionnaires to be able to show change, if there was change, in a learning organization.

Our questionnaires were administered in the original *Education for the Future* schools in October and April three years in a row. We found mostly the same results for students and parents in October and April within each year. We could see the questionnaire results change from April to October when there were changes implemented in school processes. These findings made us think that whatever perceptions students and parents have at the beginning of a school year are the same perceptions they will have at the end of the year, unless there has been some systemic change.

Staff questionnaire results are different when changes are made in the system, such as the creation of a vision or implementation of a new plan. If something different is implemented, or relationships change, teachers' responses on related items change. We find that student responses will change if teacher responses change. If teachers' responses do not change, students' responses do not change. Our current reliability quotients are .93 for the elementary student questionnaire, .97 for the secondary student questionnaire, .86 for the staff questionnaire, and .90 for the parent questionnaire.

WHERE THE ITEMS CAME FROM

The items used in the *Education for the Future* questionnaires were created from the research about student learning and what students, teachers, and parents tell us have to be in place in order for students to learn. For example, William Glasser (*The Quality School,* 1998) believes that students have to feel safe, like they belong, and have freedom, fun, and choices in their learning in order to learn. Students tell us that the one thing that has to be in place in order for them to learn is that their teacher(s) cares about them.

Figures 9.1 through 9.3 describe why the different items are used in our student, staff, and parent questionnaires, respectively.

Note: We purposefully do not use exactly the same items or questions in student, staff, and parent questionnaires. In our experience with questionnaire administration, we have found that the items or questions for each of these groups need to be different. For example, we think it is valid and important to ask students if they feel like they belong at school. It is not valid to ask parents if they think the students feel like they belong at the school— that information would be second-hand. It is valid and important to ask parents if they feel welcome at the school. It would not be appropriate to ask students if they think their parents feel welcome at the school. How does anyone know how someone else feels? We want to ask questions of the source.

Figure 9.1
EDUCATION FOR THE FUTURE STUDENT QUESTIONNAIRE

Questionnaire Items	Why We Ask These Items

At school, I feel—
  I belong.
  I am safe.
  I have fun learning.
  I have freedom at school.
  I have choices in what I learn.
	William Glasser (*The Quality School*, 1998) says students have to feel these things in order for them to learn.

I like this school. This school is good.	These statements come from the students. They think it is important that students like their school and think it is good.
My teacher cares about me. My teacher treats me with respect. My teacher thinks I will be successful. My teacher listens to my ideas. I am challenged by the work my teacher asks me to do. The work I do in class makes me think.	The number one thing that students tell us has to be in place in order for them to learn is a caring teacher(s). To students, caring means that the teacher knows, respects, and listens to them while making sure that the students are learning and actively doing challenging work. This information is consistent with the literature on dropout prevention.
My teacher is a good teacher. My teacher believes I can learn. I am recognized for good work. I know what I am supposed to be learning in my classes. Quality work is expected at my school.	Teachers want students to say that they are good teachers, that they believe the students can learn, that teachers recognize students for good work, that students know what they are supposed to be learning, and that good work is expected of students. Teachers feel these are some of the most important things that students can say about their learning that will also help them learn.
My principal cares about me.	Students asked us to add this item. They understand the importance of leadership in establishing a caring climate/culture.
I am a good student. I can be a better student. I behave well at school.	These items help students reflect on their efforts and encourage them to do better.
Students are treated fairly by teachers Students are treated fairly by the principal. Students are treated fairly by the people on recess duty (grounds supervisors).	Fair treatment is a big issue for students, especially as they get older. Often we find that the adults who are supervising the students do not have the training they need to offer balanced and respectful supervision. Students are the first to know and sometimes the last to be listened to when it comes to fair treatment, both in and out of class.
Students at my school treat me with respect. Students at my school are friendly. I have lots of friends.	These items on respect can give staffs a "heads up" on bullying and let them know what students are feeling about other students.
I have support for learning at home. My family believes I can do well in school. My family wants me to do well in school.	Students usually feel they have support for learning at home and that they are expected to do well in school. This is very interesting to teachers who feel that parents do little to help students learn at home. Perhaps teachers need to be clearer about how they help families help their children learn.

Figure 9.2
EDUCATION FOR THE FUTURE STAFF QUESTIONNAIRE

Questionnaire Items	Why We Ask These Items
I feel like I belong at this school. I feel that the staff cares about me. I feel recognized for good work. I work with people who treat me with respect. I work with people who listen if I have ideas about doing things better. I love working at this school.	These items help establish teachers' belonging at the school. If teachers do not feel like they belong or are respected, they will neither be able to focus on the needs of the students, nor will they be able to collaborate with colleagues to create a continuum of learning for all students.
I feel that learning can be fun. I feel that learning is fun at this school. Learning is fun in my classroom.	Students say they like school because it is *fun. Fun* to them means that it is challenging and worth their time. In order for the learning to be fun for students, teachers have to know how to make it *fun,* as well as challenging.
I feel intrinsically rewarded for doing my job well.	How much are teachers feeling intrinsically rewarded for doing a good job, and how much do they need external rewards? Our most effective teachers feel intrinsically rewarded for doing their jobs well.
My administrator treats me with respect. My administrator is an effective instructional leader. My administrator allows me to be an effective instructional leader. My administrator facilitates communication effectively. My administrator supports me in my work with students. My administrator supports shared decision making. My administrator is effective in helping us reach our vision.	Teachers' perceptions of the administration help us see the impact of the leader(s) in the school. Is the administrator an instructional leader, or are the teachers the only instructional leaders? Does the administrator see her/his job to help all staff implement the shared vision? We believe that helping staff implement the vision is the leader's number one job. These items also help us see the degree of support the teachers feel they receive from administrators. Teachers feel supported when there is effective communication and mutual respect.
I have the opportunity to think for myself, not just carry out instructions.	This item helps us understand how much teachers feel they are in control of their classrooms.
I have the opportunity to develop my skills.	This item helps us know if teachers feel they have support to improve their skills.
I love seeing the results of my work with students. I believe every student can learn. I love to teach.	These three statements are what the most effective teachers in the United States say about why they got into teaching. We have found when these items are high, staffs usually got into teaching for the right reasons. Almost any kind of change is possible. When these items are low for an entire staff, there is not a single plan on the planet that will be implemented without some team-building and professional learning that remind teachers about why they got into teaching in the first place.
I work effectively with special education students I work effectively with limited English speaking students. I work effectively with an ethnically/ radically diverse population of students. I work effectively with heterogeneously grouped classes. I work effectively with low-achieving students.	On an anonymous questionnaire, teachers say if they feel they work effectively with different types of students. Professional learning needs can be determined from the responses to these items.

Figure 9.2 *(Continued)*
EDUCATION FOR THE FUTURE STAFF QUESTIONNAIRE

Questionnaire Items	Why We Ask These Items
I believe student achievement can increase through differentiating instruction. I believe student achievement can increase through effective professional development related to our vision. I believe student achievement can increase through teaching to the state standards. I believe student achievement can increase through student self-assessment. I believe student achievement can increase through using ongoing student assessments related to state standards. I believe student achievement can increase through teacher use of student achievement data. I believe student achievement can increase through the use of computers. I believe student achievement can increase through providing a threat-free environment. I believe student achievement can increase through close personal relationships between students and teachers. I believe student achievement can increase through addressing student learning styles. I believe student achievement can increase through effective parent involvement. I believe student achievement can increase through partnerships with business.	As humans, we cannot act any different from what we value, believe, or perceive. When we ask teachers if they believe student achievement can increase through specific methodologies that are spelled out in the literature on effective schools, their responses essentially tell us what they are doing in their classrooms. These responses can tell staffs if the shared vision is being implemented and what professional learning might be necessary. If teachers say they do not believe student achievement can increase through strategies agreed upon, it does not mean they do not want to do them, necessarily. It often means they need more learning on the topic and to "see what it would look like if implemented in their own classroom."
The instructional program at this school is challenging. This school provides an atmosphere where every student can succeed. Quality work is expected of all students at this school. Quality work is expected of me. Quality work is expected of all the adults working at this school.	These items provide information about the feelings teachers have about the quality of work offered and provided to students and the equality of expectations. If there is a discrepancy between what teachers feel is expected of them and the other adults at the school, there probably is not a feeling of camaraderie or a chance that together they can create a continuum of learning for all students. These items could also point to a sense of fair treatment.
The vision for this school is clear. The vision for this school is shared.	The analysis of these statements show what staffs are thinking about the clarity and commitment of staffs in implementing the vision.
We have an action plan in place that can get us to our vision.	Does everyone know there is an action plan in place to implement the vision? Or did the Leadership Team create the vision and put it on the shelf? The collective results show what staffs are thinking about the plan.
This school has a good public image.	All members of the staff are responsible for the public image of the school. A good public image assists with staff morale.

Figure 9.2 *(Continued)*
EDUCATION FOR THE FUTURE STAFF QUESTIONNAIRE

Questionnaire Items	Why We Ask These Items
I think it is important to communicate often with parents. I communicate with parents often about their child's progress. I communicate with parents often about class activities.	These questions explore the discrepancy between knowing it is important to communicate with parents and actually doing it for the right reasons.
Morale is high on the part of teachers. Morale is high on the part of students. Morale is high on the part of support staff. Morale is high on the part of administrators. Teachers in this school communicate with each other to make student learning consistent across grades.	Many staffs feel that teacher morale is the lowest of any group in the school, and this is often the lowest scoring question on the staff questionnaire. If teacher morale is low, we have found that *Teachers in this school communicate with each other to make student learning consistent across grades* is also low, as well as items related to administrative communication and leadership of the vision. Teachers want to work together to create a continuum of learning that makes sense for students. If they cannot work together, a continuum of learning cannot be created.
I am clear about what my job is at this school. I feel that others are clear about what my job is at this school.	A discrepancy in responses between these two items can mean that teachers have a feeling of cognitive dissonance, or a feeling of not being valued.
The student outcomes for my class(es) are clear to me. The student outcomes for my class(es) are clear to my students.	If outcomes are not clear, there is little clarity in the school offerings or in what students should know and be able to do.

Figure 9.3
EDUCATION FOR THE FUTURE PARENT QUESTIONNAIRE

Questionnaire Items	Why We Ask These Items
I feel welcome at my student's school.	If parents do not feel welcome at the school, they will not come to the school. This answer gives us a clue about how much students feel welcome at school. Parents' comfort with the school is often symptomatic of students' comfort with the school.
I am informed about my students' progress. I know what my student's teacher expects of my student.	Parents cannot help their children learn at home if they do not know about teacher expectations or student progress.
My student is safe at school. My student is safe going to and from school. There is adequate playground supervision during school. There is adequate supervision before and after school.	One of the first issues that parents have with school is the safety of their children. The items are separated by "at school" and "going to and from school" to know the parents' major concerns about safety.
The teachers show respect for the students. The students show respect for other students.	Parents have to know that teachers and students are treating their children with respect. In most instances, if students and teachers show and feel respect for one another, bullying will not be an issue.
The school meets the social needs of the students. The school meets the academic needs of the students. The school expects quality work of its students. The school has an excellent learning environment.	In order for parents to say that the school has an excellent learning environment, parents have to know that social and academic needs of the students are being met. Parents also want their children to be engaged in quality work in an excellent learning environment.
I like the school's report card/progress report.	If parents do not understand how progress is reported to them, they cannot help their children learn at home.
I respect the school's teachers. I respect the school's principal.	Without feelings of respect for the adults at the school, parents will not get involved with the school—sometimes not even in their children's learning.
Overall, the school performs well academically. The school succeeds at preparing children for their future.	These statements give us the parents' perceptions of the quality of the school in preparing their children for the future.
The school has a good public image.	Parents' responses to this statement will coincide with the greater community's perceptions of the school's image.
The school's assessment practices are fair.	If parents do not feel the school's assessment practices are fair, they might not encourage their children to work their hardest.
My student's teacher helps me to help my student learn at home. I support my student's learning at home.	These are very important statements for understanding parent support, or lack thereof. If the parents do not know how to help their children learn, they will not be as supportive as they might be.
I feel good about myself as a parent.	Parents asked us to add this item to help understand their responses to the other questions. If I do not feel good about myself as a parent, how can I help my child learn? This could help schools know if parenting classes are something they might want to offer.

DISAGGREGATIONS

We believe that, collectively, these questionnaire items are powerful. We also know that the items become even more powerful when we disaggregate the responses. The disaggregations that we use for each questionnaire grouping follow:

Students
- Gender
- Ethnicity
- Grade
- Extracurricular participation (high school)
- Grade level when first enrolled in the school (high school)
- Plans after graduation (high school)
- School within schools identification

Staffs
- Gender (if there are appropriate numbers in each subgroup)
- Ethnicity (if there are appropriate numbers in each subgroup)
- Job Classification
- Grades and subjects taught
- Number of years of teaching
- Optional: Teaching Teams, Professional Learning Communities, etc.

Parents
- Number of children in this school
- Gender
- Number of children in the household
- Children's grades
- Native language
- Ethnic background
- Who responded (Mom, Dad, Grandparent, Guardian)
- Graduate of this school (high school)

THE SCALE

Education for the Future staff worked hard to create items that participants could respond to quickly, with results that could be displayed in meaningful ways and easily interpreted. We wanted staffs to be able to see the item results relative to each other. To do this, we piloted many different scales, including 99, 10, 7, 6, 5, 4, and 3-point scales. We ultimately and easily chose a five-point scale. Any scale that had more than five points upset the respondents—it was too fine a distinction, too hard for participants to respond. Respondents gave us less information and did not complete the questionnaire when they did not like the response options. The even numbered scales did not allow us to average the responses, and averaging provides the easiest understanding of the relationship of the responses to each other. The even numbered scales did not allow respondents to give a response that indicated half the time "yes" and half the time "no," or "just do not have an opinion at this time." The three-point scale did not discriminate enough.

Most staffs are used to results being displayed by the percentage or number of responses in agreement or disagreement with each item. Staffs struggle to find the most important and/or the least important, and do not know what to do with the information. By using averages and displaying those averages together on a line graph, as shown in Chapter 8, staffs see the degree of agreement and disagreement across items and can look at the relationship of the item content to other item content.

Our five-point response options are most often: *strongly disagree, disagree, neutral* (neither agree nor disagree), *agree,* and *strongly agree.* Sometimes we use "effective" response options in place of "agree," when appropriate for the items. These options are placed from lowest to highest, or left to right, in brain compatible order. All items are written in a positive manner so the results do not need to be inverted to understand the most positive and the most negative responses. We totally disagree with statisticians who say you need to ask questions in two different ways to make sure your respondents are telling the truth. We have found this method frustrating to respondents; plus, writing questions in a negative fashion leads to double negatives and is not brain compatible. Not using brain compatible methods will elicit results that make you think some of the respondents must have inverted the scale. However, one cannot arbitrarily invert the scale for them. The analyst must accept the responses. Typically, one could end up getting unreliable data, or have to throw out such questions, if response options are not clear.

WHAT WE HAVE LEARNED ABOUT THE EDUCATION FOR THE FUTURE QUESTIONNAIRES

People ask us all the time what we should expect to see in the results—what are typical results for different student age groups, parents, and staff members. They also ask what the results say about their learning organization. While we prefer respondents to bring their own meaning to the results, below are some of the typical findings.

Across All Respondents

What respondents, especially school staffs, like most about our questionnaires are the displays of results and the fact that the items are meaningful. By showing the average responses of each item with all other items on the same line graph, staffs can understand relationships of the items to each other, the relationship of the high responses to the lowest responses, and how the highs could provide leverage for bringing up the low item responses. This display has additional advantages: Staffs are more likely to look across all of the items before creating a plan, as opposed to picking the lowest item and then creating a plan.

The line graphs provide clear displays of disaggregated responses by different groups of respondents, e.g., males/females. The disaggregated responses have helped many staffs find issues within different student groups they did not know existed. The disaggregated responses have also shown differences in how teachers perceive their work, by the number of years of teaching, and the grades or subjects they teach.

When questionnaire items are short and understandable to all respondents in the same way, when the items progress from general to more specific, respondents are able to tell us very quickly if they agree or disagree with each of the items. We have found that it takes passion for respondents to "strongly disagree" or "strongly agree." When first looking across items, we search for those items about which students, staffs, and parents are most passionate. These are leverage for improving the low scores. When we look across the low scores, we can see relationships of these items to each other. The plan for improvement might include one major piece that will improve all items.

No matter what questionnaire you choose to use, you must always follow-up on the information to understand what respondents are saying—never assume.

Students

For the most part, the younger the students, the more in agreement they are to all the items. The older the students, the less in agreement they are with the items. Certainly there is a developmental aspect in play here; however, there are young students who are not in strong agreement with the items, and there are high school students who are in strong agreement with most of the items. We think the item responses truly reflect the learning environment. If students are treated well and they like the way they are learning, their responses will be mostly in agreement and strong agreement. If students do not have fun learning, and they do not like the way they are learning, most of their responses will be low. Students who do not feel that the teacher, or teachers, care about them or treat them fairly, have overall low responses.

Staffs

Teacher questionnaire responses show the degree to which staffs work together to create a continuum of learning for all students, if there is a clear and shared vision, and if the administrators are adding value to school processes, from the perspective of staffs. We have found that teacher morale is very closely related to how much staffs work together and are led by strong administrators, and share a vision.

Teacher questionnaire responses tell us what is being implemented and what is possible with respect to school improvement.

Parents

Parents basically report to us what their children tell them about school over the dinner table or driving to soccer or swim practice. Most often the degree of parent agreement to items matches student agreement or disagreement. However, if parents do not feel welcome at the school, or feel that they are not sure how to help their children learn, they are not involved in their children's learning.

READER CHALLENGE

What responses will you get on the Education for the Future student, staff, and parent questionnaires?

SUMMARY

In 1991, *Education for the Future* created valid and reliable questionnaires for students, staffs, and parents that continue to be used extensively today. The questionnaires have been updated over time based on feedback provided by *Education for the Future* customers. These questionnaires have shown the impact of school change on students, staff, and parents. In addition, the questionnaires have provided valid and reliable information for schools to know what needs to change in order to get different results. All of the people involved in schools, as well as those who are not directly involved, have perceptions about how well schools are doing. We can use questionnaires to discover the perceptions that people have so that we can improve the negative perceptions and build on the positive ones. Perceptual data are valuable and useful to ensure positive changes in schools and in entire districts.

We can use questionnaires to discover the perceptions that people have so that we can improve the negative perceptions and build on the positive ones.

CHAPTER 10

PULLING IT ALL TOGETHER

The purpose of this chapter is to summarize the overall process of questionnaire design, administration, and use.

Perceptions data are one of four types of data important in continuous school improvement. When used with demographics, student learning results, and school process data, perceptions data can show us what we need to do to get different results for students. Designing, administering, and using questionnaire results to improve teaching and learning includes many steps that are covered in this book and summarized in Figure 10.1. The key components of questionnaire work for continuous school improvement are highlighted below.

Perceptions data are one of the four types of data important in continuous school improvement.

Figure 10.1
KEY QUESTIONNAIRE COMPONENTS FOR CONTINUOUS IMPROVEMENT

Determine Purpose and Uses	Content and Instrument Development	Data Collection	Analyze Results	Report Results	Share and Review Results	Use Results for Continuous Improvement
Determine the purpose for the questionnaire. What do you want to learn? How will the results be used? Determine if the information already exists in some other location. If so, use that information. Establish questionnaire calendar, including timeline, person(s) responsible, costs, etc. Determine if questionnaire will be developed in-house or contracted. Begin with the end in mind. Consider all steps in the questionnaire process when planning and carrying out the tasks. Actions taken within any step impact all other steps.	Brainstorm desired concepts to capture. Conduct a literature review of content you want to capture. Disseminate findings of the literature review and create an awareness of how to develop effective questions to meet the purpose of the questionnaire. Identify subgroups for gathering and disaggregating the information. Check to see if an existing questionnaire would meet your needs. Create draft questionnaire. Determine appropriate scale. Where possible, scale items similarly to facilitate effective review of results. Pilot questionnaire. Interview pilot respondents to make sure they understand the questions in the same way. Adjust content as necessary.	Develop strategies to ensure 100% participation of staffs, students, and parents. Schedule administration—preferably in person and online—staffs first, then students, and finally parents. Parents can "take" the questionnaire on paper if they are not able to access computers. Clearly state purposes and procedures so respondents understand the importance of this data collection. Verify the data and the number of responses. Continue to administer questionnaires, if necessary, to achieve your desired response rate.	Analyze results to effectively show the best information from the questions. Disaggregate by important subgroups, even though the subgroups may not be displayed if the number in a group is small (fewer than 8). Aggregate open-ended responses.	Effectively graph results and facilitate the effective review of the results. Show items in relationship to each other to determine the common themes for what your school is doing well, and what it could do better. Provide a written report of findings.	Disseminate findings and provide staffs with time to analyze graphs and open-ended responses. Involve all stakeholders in identifying strengths, challenges, implications for the continuous improvement plan, and document questions for further exploration. Provide a written summary of the results to all respondents, in a timely fashion. Provide a summary of the results suitable for media use.	Integrate questionnaire results and findings into the school data profile; i.e., link results of questionnaires with demographic, student learning, and school process data, to eliminate contributing causes of undesirable results, to predict and ensure successes, and to effectively plan for continuous improvement. Develop an action plan based on the findings.

DETERMINE THE PURPOSE AND USES

To create a questionnaire that is useable, the first questions that must be answered during the design phase are *What is the purpose for the questionnaire, What do you want to learn,* and *How will the results be used?* The answers to these questions should guide the entire process. We need to begin with the end in mind and consider all steps in the questionnaire process when planning and carrying out the development of the questionnaire, as well as the gathering, analysis, and use of the questionnaire data. Actions taken within any step of the process can impact all other steps.

Once the purpose has been decided, the questionnaire committee will need to determine if the information already exists in some other location. If so, use that information.

If the data do not exist in another location, determine if the questionnaire will be developed in-house or contracted. Establish a questionnaire development plan, including calendar, timeline, person(s) responsible, costs, etc.

CONTENT AND INSTRUMENT DEVELOPMENT

With the purpose in mind, the questionnaire committee needs to brainstorm the desired concepts to be measured. A literature review of content may be needed to understand what information needs to be captured. Disseminate findings of the literature review and create an awareness of how to develop effective questions to meet the purpose of the questionnaire. However, before creating a new instrument, check to see if an existing questionnaire meets your needs. If there is one, use or adapt it. Creating a new questionnaire is time-consuming and difficult.

Identify the logical sources of information to answer the questions you want to use. Further, think about how you might want to disaggregate the results later, and how you want to use the information.

Create a draft questionnaire. This step is one of the hardest and longest steps of the entire questionnaire process. Draft the questions from the literature review and purpose, and then order the questions into a form that moves from general to more specific.

Determine appropriate scale. Depending upon the types of questions you plan to use, determine a scale that will get the information into a useful form. For example, if you want to graph averages later on, use an odd numbered scale with at least five points. Where possible, scale items similarly to facilitate effective review of results. Each type of scale requires a different display.

Pilot the questionnaire. When the questions and the scales have been determined, along with the ordering of the questions, pilot the questionnaire to a sample similar to the type of people you want to survey. Study the results, and interview pilot respondents to make sure they understand the questions in the same way. Adjust content as necessary. Revise the questionnaire and finalize when it seems to be gathering the data you want.

DATA COLLECTION

To collect the data from the questionnaire, develop strategies to ensure 100% participation of staff, students, and parents. For students, the questionnaire can be administered during the school day during a time when all the students are working at a computer. A staff meeting is an outstanding time to get all staff responses. Try to get parents in person if at all possible. Parent-teacher conferences are a good time. Schedule administration—preferably in person and online—staff first, then students, and finally parents. Parents can complete the questionnaire on paper if they are not comfortable or able to access computers.

To collect the data from the questionnaire, develop strategies to ensure 100% participation of staffs, students, and parents.

When administering the questionnaires, clearly state purposes and procedures so respondents understand the importance of this data collection. Make sure they know that their responses are anonymous, and that the results will be aggregated so no individual's responses can be identified.

Always verify the data and the number of responses. Continue to administer questionnaires, if necessary, to achieve your desired response rate.

ANALYZE RESULTS

Analyze results to effectively show the best information. When you can, use a comprehensive graph so the items will be displayed with each other and not in isolation. Disaggregate the results by important subgroups to check for differences. If the number in a subgroup is small (fewer than 8), that subgroup should not be displayed.

Open-ended responses can help describe the results of the multiple choice items. Open-ended items need to be aggregated, or summarized, to know the most-often written-in response.

Open-ended items need to be aggregated to know the most-often written-in response.

REPORT RESULTS

For questionnaire results to be used effectively, graph results and facilitate the review of the results. Again, show items in relationship to each other to determine the common themes for what is going well, and what needs to be improved. Provide a written report of findings.

SHARE AND REVIEW RESULTS

Disseminate a written summary of the results to all respondents, in a timely fashion, and provide staff with time to analyze graphs and open-ended responses. Involve all stakeholders in identifying strengths, challenges, implications for the school improvement plan, and document questions for further exploration. Provide a summary of the results suitable for media use.

USE RESULTS FOR SCHOOL CONTINUOUS IMPROVEMENT

Integrate questionnaire results and findings into the school data profile; i.e., link results of questionnaires with demographic, student learning, and school process data, to eliminate contributing causes of undesirable results, to predict and ensure successes, and to effectively plan for continuous improvement. Develop an action plan based on the findings.

*Do you know how you will develop a quality questionnaire,
administer it to get the highest response rate, analyze and
present the results so they can be used with other
school data for continuous improvement?*

SUMMARY

The development of a valid and reliable questionnaire is not an easy task. Many details must be taken into consideration at every step along the way, beginning with the purpose of the questionnaire and how its results will be used.

As you think through all the steps in designing and using a questionnaire, remember this—you are taking many individuals' time and energies, including your own, to put together a questionnaire and to analyze it. Think through all the steps, research the topics, and think about the people involved before you begin. Make sure you build trust so staff knows the results will not be used against them—then follow through. Treat each questionnaire as a scientific instrument, not just as a list of questions to ask people. Determine the best approach for your staff to review the data. Have fun with the review, and use the results with the demographic, student learning, and school process data to get a big picture view of your school, and then create a plan that will make a difference for students.

APPENDIX

EDUCATION FOR THE FUTURE SAMPLE QUESTIONNAIRES

On the pages that follow are *Education for the Future's* most popular student, parent, and staff questionnaires. Schools working with *Education for the Future* have used these questionnaires since 1991, and we offer them here as examples of questionnaires that work. We recommend administering them online.

Please note that these questionnaires cannot be copied and scanned as they appear in this book. They must be set-up to be scanned or to be administered online. Chapters 4 and 5 include details of questionnaire administration and analysis.

The questionnaire examples that follow include:

▼ Student (Kindergarten to Grade 3) Questionnaire

▼ Student (Grades 1 to 12) Questionnaire

▼ Student (Middle/High School) Questionnaire

▼ Parent (K-12) Questionnaire

▼ Parent (High School) Questionnaire

▼ Teaching Staff Questionnaire

▼ Staff Questionnaire

▼ School Administrators Questionnaire

▼ Alumni Questionnaire

▼ Organizational Learning Questionnaire

Education for the Future

I am in:
O Kindergarten
O First Grade
O Second Grade
O Third Grade

I am:
(fill in all that apply)
O Black (African-American)
O American Indian/
  Alaskan Native
O Asian
O White (Caucasian)
O Hispanic/Latino
O Other

I am:
O Boy
O Girl

When I am at school, I feel:

	☹	😐	☺
I belong	①	②	③
I am safe	①	②	③
I have fun learning	①	②	③
I like this school	①	②	③
This school is good	①	②	③
My teacher cares about me	①	②	③
My principal cares about me	①	②	③
My teacher is a good teacher	①	②	③
My teacher believes I can learn	①	②	③
The work I do in class makes me think	①	②	③
I know what I am supposed to be learning in my classes	①	②	③
I am a good student	①	②	③
I can be a better student	①	②	③
I behave well at school	①	②	③
Students at my school are friendly	①	②	③
I have lots of friends	①	②	③
My family believes I can do well in school	①	②	③
My family wants me to do well in school	①	②	③

Page 1 of 2 *(Continued)* ⟶

Education for the Future

What do you like about this school?

What do you wish was different at this school?

Education for the Future

Students

I am in:
- ○ 1st Grade
- ○ 2nd Grade
- ○ 3rd Grade
- ○ 4th Grade
- ○ 5th Grade
- ○ 6th Grade
- ○ 7th Grade
- ○ 8th Grade
- ○ 9th Grade
- ○ 10th Grade
- ○ 11th Grade
- ○ 12th Grade

I am:
(fill in all that apply)
- ○ Black (African-American)
- ○ American Indian/ Alaskan Native
- ○ Asian
- ○ White (Caucasian)
- ○ Hispanic/Latino
- ○ Other

I am:
- ○ Boy
- ○ Girl

When I am at school, I feel:	Strongly Disagree	Disagree	Neutral	Agree	Strongly Agree
I belong	①	②	③	④	⑤
I am safe	①	②	③	④	⑤
I have fun learning	①	②	③	④	⑤
I like this school	①	②	③	④	⑤
This school is good	①	②	③	④	⑤
I have freedom at school	①	②	③	④	⑤
I have choices in the way I learn	①	②	③	④	⑤
My teacher treats me with respect	①	②	③	④	⑤
My teacher cares about me	①	②	③	④	⑤
My teacher thinks I will be successful	①	②	③	④	⑤
My teacher listens to my ideas	①	②	③	④	⑤
My principal cares about me	①	②	③	④	⑤
My teacher is a good teacher	①	②	③	④	⑤
My teacher believes I can learn	①	②	③	④	⑤
I am recognized for good work	①	②	③	④	⑤
I am challenged by the work my teacher asks me to do	①	②	③	④	⑤
The work I do in class makes me think	①	②	③	④	⑤
I know what I am supposed to be learning in my classes	①	②	③	④	⑤
I am a good student	①	②	③	④	⑤
I can be a better student	①	②	③	④	⑤
Working hard will make me do well in school	①	②	③	④	⑤
Very good work is expected at my school	①	②	③	④	⑤
I behave well at school	①	②	③	④	⑤
Students are treated fairly by teachers	①	②	③	④	⑤
Students are treated fairly by the principal	①	②	③	④	⑤
Students are treated fairly by campus supervisors	①	②	③	④	⑤
Students at my school treat me with respect	①	②	③	④	⑤
I am safe from bullies	①	②	③	④	⑤
Students at my school are friendly	①	②	③	④	⑤
I have lots of friends	①	②	③	④	⑤
I have support for learning at home	①	②	③	④	⑤
My family believes I can do well in school	①	②	③	④	⑤
My family wants me to do well in school	①	②	③	④	⑤

Page 1 of 2 *(Continued)* ➡

Education for the Future

Students

What do you like about this school?

What do you wish was different at this school?

Education for the Future

Middle/High School Students

NOTE: This PDF file is for content review purposes only—*not* intended for use in questionnaire administration. For more information about administering and analyzing *Education for the Future* questionnaires, please visit: *http://eff.csuchico.edu/questionnaire_resources/*.

	Strongly Disagree	Disagree	Neutral	Agree	Strongly Agree
I feel safe at this school	①	②	③	④	⑤
I feel like I belong at this school	①	②	③	④	⑤
I feel challenged at this school	①	②	③	④	⑤
I have opportunities to choose my own projects	①	②	③	④	⑤
I feel that I am in charge of what I learn	①	②	③	④	⑤
Teachers encourage me to assess the quality of my own work	①	②	③	④	⑤
This school is preparing me well for what I want to do after high school	①	②	③	④	⑤
My teachers treat me fairly	①	②	③	④	⑤
My school administrators treat me fairly	①	②	③	④	⑤
My campus supervisors treat me fairly	①	②	③	④	⑤
The office staff treat me fairly	①	②	③	④	⑤
Other students at this school treat me fairly	①	②	③	④	⑤
The work at this school is challenging	①	②	③	④	⑤
I find what I learn in school to be relevant to real life	①	②	③	④	⑤
I feel successful at school	①	②	③	④	⑤
This school is fun	①	②	③	④	⑤
I like this school	①	②	③	④	⑤
This is a good school	①	②	③	④	⑤
I like the students at this school	①	②	③	④	⑤
Students at this school like me	①	②	③	④	⑤
I like to learn	①	②	③	④	⑤
Doing well in school makes me feel good about myself	①	②	③	④	⑤
Working hard will make me do well in school	①	②	③	④	⑤
I am doing my best in school	①	②	③	④	⑤
Participating in extracurricular activities is important to me	①	②	③	④	⑤

Page 1 of 3 *(Continued)* ➡

Education for the Future

Middle/High School Students

	Strongly Disagree	Disagree	Neutral	Agree	Strongly Agree

My teachers:

expect students to do their best	①	②	③	④	⑤
expect me to do my best	①	②	③	④	⑤
are understanding when students have personal problems	①	②	③	④	⑤
set high standards for learning in their classes	①	②	③	④	⑤
help me gain confidence in my ability to learn	①	②	③	④	⑤
know me well	①	②	③	④	⑤
care about me	①	②	③	④	⑤
make learning fun	①	②	③	④	⑤
are excited about the subjects they teach	①	②	③	④	⑤
give me individual attention when I need it	①	②	③	④	⑤

In my classes, time is spent:

listening to the teacher talk	①	②	③	④	⑤
in whole class discussions	①	②	③	④	⑤
working in small groups	①	②	③	④	⑤
answering questions from a book or worksheet	①	②	③	④	⑤
working on projects or research	①	②	③	④	⑤
doing work that I find meaningful	①	②	③	④	⑤
using computers	①	②	③	④	⑤

I learn well when:

I am working on projects or research	①	②	③	④	⑤
the teacher is leading a discussion with the whole class	①	②	③	④	⑤
I am working in a small group	①	②	③	④	⑤
I am working by myself	①	②	③	④	⑤

I feel ready for the real world, with reference to:

my ability to write	①	②	③	④	⑤
my ability to read	①	②	③	④	⑤
my ability with mathematics	①	②	③	④	⑤
my ability to process information	①	②	③	④	⑤
my presentation skills	①	②	③	④	⑤
my technology skills	①	②	③	④	⑤
my ability to learn on my own outside of a classroom	①	②	③	④	⑤

Page 2 of 3 *(Continued)* ➤

Education for the Future

Middle/High School Students

What do you like about this school?

What do you wish was different at this school?

Student Demographic Data

I am: (fill in all that apply)
○ Black (African-American)
○ American Indian/Alaskan Native
○ Asian
○ White (Caucasian)
○ Filipino
○ Hispanic/Latino
○ Middle Eastern
○ Pacific Islander
○ Other _____

I am in the:
○ 6th Grade
○ 7th Grade
○ 8th Grade
○ 9th Grade
○ 10th Grade
○ 11th Grade
○ 12th Grade

I am:
○ Female
○ Male

I participate in: (fill in all that apply)
○ Athletics (includes Cheerleading/Flag Team)
○ School Clubs
○ Instrumental Music
○ Vocal Music
○ Drama
○ Speech/Debate
○ Not connected to any school club or
   regular extracurricular activity

I came to this school as a:
○ 6th Grader   ○ Freshman
○ 7th Grader   ○ Sophomore
○ 8th Grader   ○ Junior
                  ○ Senior

**Immediately after graduation, I plan to:
(fill in all that apply)**
○ Go to a 2-year community college
○ Go to a 4-year college
○ Enter a training or apprenticeship program
○ Get a full-time job
○ Join the military
○ Get married
○ Other _____

Page 3 of 3

Education for the Future

Parents

NOTE: This PDF file is for content review purposes only—*not* **intended for use in questionnaire administration. For more information about administering and analyzing** *Education for the Future* **questionnaires, please visit:** *http://eff.csuchico.edu/questionnaire_resources/.*

	Strongly Disagree	Disagree	Neutral	Agree	Strongly Agree
I feel welcome at my child's school	①	②	③	④	⑤
I am informed about my child's progress	①	②	③	④	⑤
I know what my child's teacher expects of my child	①	②	③	④	⑤
My child is safe at school	①	②	③	④	⑤
My child is safe going to and from school	①	②	③	④	⑤
There is adequate supervision during school	①	②	③	④	⑤
There is adequate supervision before and after school	①	②	③	④	⑤
Teachers show respect for the students	①	②	③	④	⑤
Students show respect for other students	①	②	③	④	⑤
The school meets the social needs of the students	①	②	③	④	⑤
The school meets the academic needs of the students	①	②	③	④	⑤
The school expects quality work of its students	①	②	③	④	⑤
The school has an excellent learning environment	①	②	③	④	⑤
I know how well my child is progressing in school	①	②	③	④	⑤
I like the school's report cards/progress report	①	②	③	④	⑤
I respect the school's teachers	①	②	③	④	⑤
I respect the school's principal	①	②	③	④	⑤
Overall, the school performs well academically	①	②	③	④	⑤
The school succeeds at preparing children for future work	①	②	③	④	⑤
The school has a good public image	①	②	③	④	⑤
The school's assessment practices are fair	①	②	③	④	⑤
My child's teacher helps me to help my child learn at home	①	②	③	④	⑤
I support my child's learning at home	①	②	③	④	⑤
I feel good about myself as a parent	①	②	③	④	⑤

Children's grades:
○ Kindergarten
○ First Grade
○ Second Grade
○ Third Grade
○ Fourth Grade
○ Fifth Grade
○ Sixth Grade
○ Seventh Grade
○ Eighth Grade
○ Ninth Grade
○ Tenth Grade
○ Eleventh Grade
○ Twelfth Grade

Number of children in this school:
① ② ③ ④ ⑤ ⑥ ⑦ ⑧ ⑨

My native language is:
○ Chinese
○ Eastern European
○ English
○ Japanese
○ Korean
○ Spanish
○ Vietnamese
○ Other _____

Number of children in the household:
① ② ③ ④ ⑤ ⑥ ⑦ ⑧ ⑨

Ethnic background:
(fill in all that apply)
○ Black (African-American)
○ American Indian/Alaskan Native
○ Asian
○ White (Caucasian)
○ Hispanic/Latino
○ Other _____

Responding:
○ Mother
○ Father
○ Guardian
○ Other

Page 1 of 2 *(Continued)* ➡

Parents

What are the strengths of this school?

What needs to be improved?

Education for the Future

High School Parents

NOTE: This PDF file is for content review purposes only—*not* intended for use in questionnaire administration. For more information about administering and analyzing *Education for the Future* questionnaires, please visit: *http://eff.csuchico.edu/questionnaire_resources/.*

	Strongly Disagree	Disagree	Neutral	Agree	Strongly Agree
I feel welcome at my child's school	①	②	③	④	⑤
My child is safe at school	①	②	③	④	⑤
My child is safe going to and from school	①	②	③	④	⑤
There is adequate supervision during school	①	②	③	④	⑤
There is adequate supervision before and after school	①	②	③	④	⑤
I am informed about my child's progress at school	①	②	③	④	⑤
My calls to the school are returned in a timely manner	①	②	③	④	⑤
I know what my child's teachers expect of my child	①	②	③	④	⑤
My child knows what his/her teachers expect of him/her	①	②	③	④	⑤
New students receive adequate orientation to the school and the programs offered	①	②	③	④	⑤
The school provides adequate information to students about attending college after graduation	①	②	③	④	⑤
The school provides adequate information about non-college options after graduation	①	②	③	④	⑤
The school provides an adequate calendar of school activities	①	②	③	④	⑤
The school clearly communicates how parent volunteers can help	①	②	③	④	⑤
Parent volunteers are made to feel appreciated	①	②	③	④	⑤
Parent volunteers are vital to the school community	①	②	③	④	⑤
I respect the school's teachers	①	②	③	④	⑤
I respect the school's principal	①	②	③	④	⑤
Students are treated fairly by the teachers	①	②	③	④	⑤
Students are treated fairly by administration	①	②	③	④	⑤
Students are treated fairly by other students	①	②	③	④	⑤
The school meets the social needs of the students	①	②	③	④	⑤
The school meets the academic needs of the students	①	②	③	④	⑤
The school expects quality work of its students	①	②	③	④	⑤
The school's assessment practices are fair	①	②	③	④	⑤
Overall, the school performs well academically	①	②	③	④	⑤
There is adequate recognition of student successes	①	②	③	④	⑤
The school succeeds at preparing its students for future work	①	②	③	④	⑤
Teachers help me know how to support my child's learning at home	①	②	③	④	⑤
I support my child's learning at home	①	②	③	④	⑤
Overall, the school has a good public image	①	②	③	④	⑤
I would recommend this school to other families	①	②	③	④	⑤

Page 1 of 2 *(Continued)* ➡

Education for the Future

High School Parents

What are the strengths of this school?

What needs to be improved?

Demographics

Number of children in this school:
① ② ③ ④ ⑤ ⑥ ⑦ ⑧ ⑨

Number of children in the household:
① ② ③ ④ ⑤ ⑥ ⑦ ⑧ ⑨

Children's grades:
○ Kindergarten
○ First Grade
○ Second Grade
○ Third Grade
○ Fourth Grade
○ Fifth Grade
○ Sixth Grade
○ Seventh Grade
○ Eighth Grade
○ Ninth Grade
○ Tenth Grade
○ Eleventh Grade
○ Twelfth Grade

My native language is:
○ Chinese
○ Eastern European
○ English
○ Japanese
○ Korean
○ Spanish
○ Vietnamese
○ Other _____

Ethnic background:
(fill in all that apply)
○ Black (African-American
○ American Indian/Alaskan Native
○ Asian
○ White (Caucasian)
○ Hispanic/Latino
○ Other _____

I am a graduate of this high school:
○ Yes
○ No

Responding:
○ Mother
○ Father
○ Guardian
○ Other

Education for the Future

Teaching Staff

NOTE: This PDF file is for content review purposes only—*not* intended for use in questionnaire administration. For more information about administering and analyzing *Education for the Future* questionnaires, please visit: *http://eff.csuchico.edu/questionnaire_resources/*.

	Strongly Disagree	Disagree	Neutral	Agree	Strongly Agree

(1) I feel:

	SD	D	N	A	SA
like I belong at this school	①	②	③	④	⑤
that the staff cares about me	①	②	③	④	⑤
that learning can be fun	①	②	③	④	⑤
that learning is fun at this school	①	②	③	④	⑤
recognized for good work	①	②	③	④	⑤
intrinsically rewarded for doing my job well	①	②	③	④	⑤
clear about what my job is at this school	①	②	③	④	⑤
that others are clear about what my job is at this school	①	②	③	④	⑤

(2) I work with people who:

	SD	D	N	A	SA
treat me with respect	①	②	③	④	⑤
respect each other	①	②	③	④	⑤
collaborate with each other to make student learning consistent across grade levels	①	②	③	④	⑤
are committed to continuous improvement	①	②	③	④	⑤
provide one another feedback on their teaching	①	②	③	④	⑤

(3) My administrators:

	SD	D	N	A	SA
treat me with respect	①	②	③	④	⑤
are effective instructional leaders	①	②	③	④	⑤
facilitate communication effectively	①	②	③	④	⑤
support me in my work with students	①	②	③	④	⑤
support shared decision making	①	②	③	④	⑤
allow me to be an effective instructional leader	①	②	③	④	⑤
are effective in helping us reach our vision	①	②	③	④	⑤
actively encourage staff to collaborate	①	②	③	④	⑤

(4) I believe student achievement can increase through:

	SD	D	N	A	SA
differentiating instruction	①	②	③	④	⑤
effective professional development related to our vision	①	②	③	④	⑤
teaching to the state standards	①	②	③	④	⑤
the use of computers	①	②	③	④	⑤
providing a threat-free environment	①	②	③	④	⑤
close personal relationships between students and teachers	①	②	③	④	⑤
addressing student learning styles	①	②	③	④	⑤
effective parent involvement	①	②	③	④	⑤
using ongoing student assessments related to state standards	①	②	③	④	⑤
student self-assessments	①	②	③	④	⑤
teacher use of student achievement data	①	②	③	④	⑤

(5) I love:

	SD	D	N	A	SA
working at this school	①	②	③	④	⑤
seeing the results of my work with students	①	②	③	④	⑤
to teach	①	②	③	④	⑤

Page 1 of 6 *(Continued)* ➤

Education for the Future

Teaching Staff

	Strongly Disagree	Disagree	Neutral	Agree	Strongly Agree

(6) I believe:

	Strongly Disagree	Disagree	Neutral	Agree	Strongly Agree
every student can learn	①	②	③	④	⑤
the instructional program at this school is challenging	①	②	③	④	⑤
this school provides an atmosphere where every student can succeed	①	②	③	④	⑤
quality work is expected of all students at this school	①	②	③	④	⑤
quality work is expected of me	①	②	③	④	⑤
quality work is expected of all the adults working at this school	①	②	③	④	⑤
the vision for this school is clear	①	②	③	④	⑤
the vision for this school is shared	①	②	③	④	⑤
we have an action plan in place which will get us to our vision	①	②	③	④	⑤
this school has a good public image	①	②	③	④	⑤
it is important to communicate often with parents	①	②	③	④	⑤
I communicate with parents often about their child's progress	①	②	③	④	⑤
student outcomes for my class(es) are clear to me	①	②	③	④	⑤
student outcomes for my class(es) are clear to my students	①	②	③	④	⑤
learning is fun in my classroom	①	②	③	④	⑤

(7) I work effectively with:

	Strongly Disagree	Disagree	Neutral	Agree	Strongly Agree
students with learning disabilities	①	②	③	④	⑤
English learners	①	②	③	④	⑤
ethnically/racially diverse students	①	②	③	④	⑤
students who live in poverty	①	②	③	④	⑤
low-achieving students	①	②	③	④	⑤

(8) Morale is high on the part of:

	Strongly Disagree	Disagree	Neutral	Agree	Strongly Agree
teachers	①	②	③	④	⑤
students	①	②	③	④	⑤
support staff	①	②	③	④	⑤
our school administrators	①	②	③	④	⑤

Page 2 of 6 *(Continued)* ➡

Education for the Future

Teaching Staff

Standards Assessment for
Elementary School Teachers only *(Middle/High Teachers skip to question #14)*

*The analysis of the following questions will inform staff of where your school is in the process of implementing state standards, and what support structures are needed to make the effective implementation of standards possible. Only **group** results will be used. Individuals will not be identified. It is okay if you do not know a set of standards now. This assessment will show your school's progress over time. Please answer the questions to the best of your ability, with the first answers that come to mind. Use N/A when the question is not applicable to your situation. Completely fill in the circle, using the scale to the right. Thank you!*

(9) **How well do you know the state standards at your grade level(s) for the following content areas?**

	Just know they exist	Have skimmed	Have read at least once	Have read in-depth	Am very knowledgeable
English/Language Arts	①	②	③	④	⑤
Mathematics	①	②	③	④	⑤
Science	①	②	③	④	⑤
Social Studies	①	②	③	④	⑤
Technology	①	②	③	④	⑤

(10) **How well do you know the state standards just below your grade level(s) for the following content areas?**

	Just know they exist	Have skimmed	Have read at least once	Have read in-depth	Am very knowledgeable
English/Language Arts	①	②	③	④	⑤
Mathematics	①	②	③	④	⑤
Science	①	②	③	④	⑤
Social Studies	①	②	③	④	⑤
Technology	①	②	③	④	⑤

(11) **How well do you know the state standards just above your grade level(s) for the following content areas?**

	Just know they exist	Have skimmed	Have read at least once	Have read in-depth	Am very knowledgeable
English/Language Arts	①	②	③	④	⑤
Mathematics	①	②	③	④	⑤
Science	①	②	③	④	⑤
Social Studies	①	②	③	④	⑤
Technology	①	②	③	④	⑤

(12) **How well would you say you know what it would look like, sound like, and feel like if you were teaching to the standards 100% of the time?**

	Not at All	Little Bit	Getting There	Well	Extremely Well
English/Language Arts	①	②	③	④	⑤
Mathematics	①	②	③	④	⑤
Science	①	②	③	④	⑤
Social Studies	①	②	③	④	⑤
Technology	①	②	③	④	⑤

(13) **How much of the time are you implementing the standards in your classroom for the following content areas?**

	0%	25%	50%	75%	100%
English/Language Arts	①	②	③	④	⑤
Mathematics	①	②	③	④	⑤
Science	①	②	③	④	⑤
Social Studies	①	②	③	④	⑤
Technology	①	②	③	④	⑤

Page 3 of 6 *(Continued)* ➤

Education for the Future

Standards Assessment for
Middle and High School Teachers only

*The analysis of the following questions will inform staff of where your school is in the process of implementing state standards, and what support structures are needed to make the effective implementation of standards possible. Only **group** results will be used. Individuals will not be identified. It is okay if you do not know a set of standards now. This assessment will show your school's progress over time. Please answer the questions to the best of your ability, with the first answers that come to mind. Use N/A when the question is not applicable to your situation. Completely fill in the circle, using the scale to the right. Thank you!*

	Just know they exist	Have skimmed	Have read at least once	Have read in-depth	Am very knowledgeable
(14) How well do you know the state standards for your grade level(s) and content areas?	①	②	③	④	⑤
(15) How well do you know the state standards for your content area(s) that precede your grade level(s)?	①	②	③	④	⑤
(16) How well do you know the state standards for your content area(s) that follow your grade level(s)?	①	②	③	④	⑤
(17) For those of you who teach upper grades, how well do you know content expectations students will encounter in higher education?	①	②	③	④	⑤

	Not at All	Little Bit	Getting There	Well	Extremely Well
(18) How well would you say you know what it would look like, sound like, and feel like if you were teaching to the standards 100% of the time?	①	②	③	④	⑤

Standards Assessment for
ALL Teachers

(19) How much would each of the following help you to better know the standards for your grade level(s)?

	Not at All	Probably Not	Not Sure	A Lot	A Great Deal
Grade-level meetings about standards	①	②	③	④	⑤
Cross-grade-level meetings about standards	①	②	③	④	⑤
Schoolwide meetings about standards	①	②	③	④	⑤
Professional development on how to teach to the standards	①	②	③	④	⑤
Feedback from classroom observations	①	②	③	④	⑤
Demonstration lessons	①	②	③	④	⑤
Peer coaching	①	②	③	④	⑤
Other	①	②	③	④	⑤

(20) Which of the following statements describes how you use standards to design instruction?
(Select one statement that best applies.)

I teach the curriculum and instructional strategies our school/district has adopted	○
I follow the textbooks, and I believe they are aligned to the state standards	○
I am pretty sure my instructional strategies are already aligned to the state standards	○
I take my existing instructional plans and indicate where the standards are being taught	○
I study the standards and create instruction to take students from where they are to where the standards say they should be by the end of the year	○
I study the standards, determine outcomes related to the standards, frequently assess where students are with respect to the standards, and adapt my lesson plans to create instruction to take students to where they need to be by the end of the year	○
I teach the standards through ongoing assessments	○

Page 4 of 6 *(Continued)* ➡

FROM QUESTIONS TO ACTIONS

Education for the Future

Teaching Staff

Standards Assessment for ALL Teachers

(21) What percentage of your students do you think will meet the standards by the end of the school year?
(Select the option that best applies.)

○ 0%   ○ 11–20%   ○ 31–40%   ○ 51–60%   ○ 71–80%   ○ 91–100%
○ 1–10%   ○ 21–30%   ○ 41–50%   ○ 61–70%   ○ 81–90%

(22) What do you do when your students do not learn the standards?
(Select *all* the boxes that apply and add other strategies, as appropriate.)

○ I reteach the content
○ I reteach the content, in different ways
○ I adapt my instructional strategies to the learning styles of individual students
○ After reteaching, I assess the students in different ways
○ I get help from others in the school, such as colleagues and/or specialists
○ I move on to make sure the curriculum gets covered
○ I cannot make a student learn
○ Other _____

(23) How much support do you receive from your school administrators to ensure that:

	No Support	Hardly Any	There is a system for support	Good Support	Continuous Support
you are teaching to the standards	①	②	③	④	⑤
your students are learning the standards	①	②	③	④	⑤
all teachers at your grade level/content area are teaching to the *same* standards	①	②	③	④	⑤
teachers across grade levels are teaching to standards	①	②	③	④	⑤
teachers across grade levels are using the standards to build a continuum of learning that makes sense for all students	①	②	③	④	⑤
teachers are using formative assessments to verify student mastery of standards	①	②	③	④	⑤

(24) How much support do you receive from your colleagues to ensure that:

	No Support	Hardly Any	There is a system for support	Good Support	Continuous Support
you are teaching to the standards	①	②	③	④	⑤
your students are learning the standards	①	②	③	④	⑤
all teachers at your grade level are teaching to the *same* standards	①	②	③	④	⑤
teachers across grade levels are teaching to standards	①	②	③	④	⑤
teachers across grade levels are using the standards to build a continuum of learning that makes sense for all students	①	②	③	④	⑤
teachers are using formative assessments to verify student mastery of standards	①	②	③	④	⑤

	Not at All	Little Bit	Getting There	Believe	Strongly Believe
(25) To what extent do you believe teachers and instructional staff can make the necessary changes to improve student learning?	①	②	③	④	⑤
(26) To what extent do you believe school leadership can facilitate the necessary changes to improve student learning?	①	②	③	④	⑤

	Not at All	Little Bit	Getting There	Committed	Strongly Committed
(27) How committed are you to making necessary changes to improve student learning?	①	②	③	④	⑤

Education for the Future

Teaching Staff

What would it take to improve student learning in this school?

What are the strengths of this school?

What needs to be improved?

Demographic Data

For each item, please select the description that applies to you. These demographic data are used for summary analyses; some descriptions will not be reported if groups are so small that individuals can be identified.

What grade level(s) do you teach?
(Mark all that apply.)

○ Pre K
○ Kindergarten
○ Grade 1
○ Grade 2
○ Grade 3
○ Grade 4
○ Grade 5
○ Grades 6
○ Grade 7-8
○ Grade 9-12

I am a(n):
○ Classroom Teacher
○ Instructional Assistant
○ Certificated Staff
　(other than a classroom teacher)
○ Classified Staff
　(other than an instructional assistant)

How long have you been a teacher?
○ 1st Year
○ 2–3 Years
○ 4–6 Years
○ 7–10 Years
○ 11–14 Years
○ 15–20 Years
○ 21–25 Years
○ 26+ Years

What content do you teach?
(Mark all that apply.)

○ Elementary
○ English/Language Arts
○ Mathematics
○ Science
○ Social Studies
○ Technology
○ Foreign Language
○ The Arts
○ Physical Education/Health
○ Special Education
○ Vocational Education
○ Industrial Education
○ Other _____

What are your teaching qualifications?
(Mark all that apply.)
○ Emergency Credential
○ Elementary Credential
○ Middle Credential
○ Secondary Credential
○ Special Education
○ Intervention Specialist
○ Literacy Specialist/Coach
○ Math Specialist/Coach
○ Classroom Instructional Assistant
○ Other _____

Thank you!

Page 6 of 6 *(Continued)* ➡

Education for the Future

Staff

NOTE: This PDF file is for content review purposes only—*not* intended for use in questionnaire administration. For more information about administering and analyzing *Education for the Future* questionnaires, please visit: *http://eff.csuchico.edu/questionnaire_resources/*.

Demographic data, which is used for summary analysis, will not be reported if individuals can be identified.

Ethnicity:
(fill in all that apply)
○ Black (African-American)
○ American Indian
○ Asian
○ White (Caucasian)
○ Latino/Hispanic
○ Other

I am a(n):
○ classroom teacher
○ instructional assistant
○ certificated staff
   (other than a classroom teacher)
○ classified staff
   (other than an instructional assistant)

Items for teachers only:
I teach:
○ pre-kindergarten
○ primary grades
○ upper elementary grades
○ middle school grades
○ high school grades 9-10
○ high school grades 11-12

I have been teaching:
○ 1-3 years
○ 4-6 years
○ 7-10 years
○ 11 or more years

Response scale: Strongly Disagree (1), Disagree (2), Neutral (3), Agree (4), Strongly Agree (5)

I feel:

	SD	D	N	A	SA
like I belong at this school	①	②	③	④	⑤
that the staff cares about me	①	②	③	④	⑤
that learning can be fun	①	②	③	④	⑤
that learning is fun at this school	①	②	③	④	⑤
recognized for good work	①	②	③	④	⑤
intrinsically rewarded for doing my job well	①	②	③	④	⑤
clear about what my job is at this school	①	②	③	④	⑤
that others are clear about what my job is at this school	①	②	③	④	⑤

I work with people who:

	SD	D	N	A	SA
treat me with respect	①	②	③	④	⑤
listen if I have ideas about doing things better	①	②	③	④	⑤

My administrators:

	SD	D	N	A	SA
treat me with respect	①	②	③	④	⑤
are effective instructional leaders	①	②	③	④	⑤
facilitate communication effectively	①	②	③	④	⑤
support me in my work with students	①	②	③	④	⑤
support shared decision making	①	②	③	④	⑤
allow me to be an effective instructional leader	①	②	③	④	⑤
are effective in helping us reach our vision	①	②	③	④	⑤

I have the opportunity to:

	SD	D	N	A	SA
develop my skills	①	②	③	④	⑤
think for myself, not just carry out instructions	①	②	③	④	⑤

I believe student achievement can increase through:

	SD	D	N	A	SA
differentiating instruction	①	②	③	④	⑤
effective professional development related to our vision	①	②	③	④	⑤
integrating instruction across the curriculum	①	②	③	④	⑤
teaching to the state standards	①	②	③	④	⑤
the use of computers	①	②	③	④	⑤
the use of varied technologies	①	②	③	④	⑤
providing a threat-free environment	①	②	③	④	⑤
close personal relationships between students and teachers	①	②	③	④	⑤
addressing student learning styles	①	②	③	④	⑤
effective parent involvement	①	②	③	④	⑤
using ongoing student assessments related to state standards	①	②	③	④	⑤
student self-assessments	①	②	③	④	⑤
teacher use of student achievement data	①	②	③	④	⑤

I love:

	SD	D	N	A	SA
working at this school	①	②	③	④	⑤
seeing the results of my work with students	①	②	③	④	⑤

Page 1 of 3 *(Continued)* ➡

Education for the Future

	Strongly Disagree	Disagree	Neutral	Agree	Strongly Agree

I believe:

every student can learn	①	②	③	④	⑤
the instructional program at this school is challenging	①	②	③	④	⑤
this school provides an atmosphere where every student can succeed	①	②	③	④	⑤
quality work is expected of all students at this school	①	②	③	④	⑤
quality work is expected of me	①	②	③	④	⑤
quality work is expected of all the adults working at this school	①	②	③	④	⑤
the vision for this school is clear	①	②	③	④	⑤
the vision for this school is shared	①	②	③	④	⑤
we have an action plan in place which can get us to our vision	①	②	③	④	⑤
this school has a good public image	①	②	③	④	⑤
it is important to communicate often with parents	①	②	③	④	⑤
I communicate with parents often about their child's progress	①	②	③	④	⑤
I communicate with parents often about class activities	①	②	③	④	⑤

I work effectively with:

special education students	①	②	③	④	⑤
English learners	①	②	③	④	⑤
ethnically/racially diverse students	①	②	③	④	⑤
students who live in poverty	①	②	③	④	⑤
low-achieving students	①	②	③	④	⑤

Morale is high on the part of:

teachers	①	②	③	④	⑤
students	①	②	③	④	⑤
support staff	①	②	③	④	⑤
administrators	①	②	③	④	⑤

Items for teachers and instructional assistants only:

Student outcomes for my class(es) are clear to me	①	②	③	④	⑤
Student outcomes for my class(es) are clear to my students	①	②	③	④	⑤
Teachers in this school communicate with each other to make student learning consistent across grades	①	②	③	④	⑤
I know the state standards	①	②	③	④	⑤
I teach to the state standards	①	②	③	④	⑤
Learning is fun in my classroom	①	②	③	④	⑤
I love to teach	①	②	③	④	⑤

Page 2 of 3 (Continued) ➜

Education for the Future

What are the strengths of this school?

What needs to be improved?

Education for the Future

School Administrators

NOTE: This PDF file is for content review purposes only—*not* intended for use in questionnaire administration. For more information about administering and analyzing *Education for the Future* questionnaires, please visit: *http://eff.csuchico.edu/questionnaire_resources/*.

	Strongly Disagree	Disagree	Neutral	Agree	Strongly Agree
I am a valued member of this School District	①	②	③	④	⑤
I am able to participate meaningfully in District decisions that impact my responsibilities	①	②	③	④	⑤
I am able to work with District leadership to generate special resources when I need them	①	②	③	④	⑤
I am allowed to be an effective leader in my school	①	②	③	④	⑤
I am encouraged to find unique solutions to issues in my school	①	②	③	④	⑤
I clearly understand the specifics of what I am held accountable for in performance reviews	①	②	③	④	⑤
I enjoy my job	①	②	③	④	⑤
I understand what is expected of me in my role	①	②	③	④	⑤
Others in the District have the same understanding of the nature of my role that I have	①	②	③	④	⑤
People in the District can explain the District's vision	①	②	③	④	⑤
People in the District respect me	①	②	③	④	⑤
Principals in the District generally like what they do here.	①	②	③	④	⑤
The District leadership cares about me	①	②	③	④	⑤
The District leadership trusts my judgment	①	②	③	④	⑤
The District provides an organizational climate in which all schools can succeed	①	②	③	④	⑤
The District strategic plan will lead us to make our vision a reality	①	②	③	④	⑤
There are opportunities for me to develop my skills	①	②	③	④	⑤
There is a District-level strategic plan in place	①	②	③	④	⑤
As a rule, District leadership requires that I use specific strategies to accomplish District goals in my school	①	②	③	④	⑤
District leadership provides adequate resources for me to get my job done effectively	①	②	③	④	⑤
District leadership provides me with direction	①	②	③	④	⑤
District leadership supports my decisions	①	②	③	④	⑤
Everyone who works in this District is expected to deliver high quality work	①	②	③	④	⑤
Good work is consistently recognized in this District	①	②	③	④	⑤

Page 1 of 2 *(Continued)* ➡

Education for the Future

School Administrators

What are the most effective things that the District does to facilitate your effectiveness?

What are the least effective things that the District does in relation to your effectiveness?

What should the District be doing, that it is not doing currently, to help make you more effective?

Administrator Demographic Data

Demographic data, which is used for summary analysis, will not be reported if individuals can be identified.

Ethnicity: *(fill in all that apply)*
- O Black (African-American)
- O American Indian/Alaskan Native
- O Asian
- O White (Caucasian)
- O Hispanic/Latino
- O Other _____

Gender:
- O Female
- O Male

I have been in my current position:
- O 1st Year
- O 2–3 Years
- O 4–6 Years
- O 7–10 Years
- O 11–14 Years
- O 15–20 Years
- O 21–25 Years
- O 26+ Years

I am a(n):
- O Elementary Assistant Principal
- O Elementary Principal
- O Middle School Assistant Principal
- O Middle School Principal
- O High School Assistant Principal
- O High School Principal
- O Other School Administrator _____
- O District Administrator
- O Specify: _____

I have been an administrator for:
- O 1st Year
- O 2–3 Years
- O 4–6 Years
- O 7–10 Years
- O 11–14 Years
- O 15–20 Years
- O 21–25 Years
- O 26+ Years

Education for the Future

NOTE: This PDF file is for content review purposes only—
not intended for use in questionnaire administration.
For more information about administering and analyzing
Education for the Future questionnaires, please visit:
http://eff.csuchico.edu/questionnaire_resources/.

Section I: Background Information

Gender:
O Male
O Female

Age:
O 18 and under
O 19-20 O 25-26
O 21-22 O 27-28
O 23-24 O 29-30

Ethnicity:
O Black (African-American)
O American Indian/Alaskan Native
O Asian
O White (Caucasian)
O Filipino
O Hispanic/Latino
O Middle Eastern
O Pacific Islander
O Other _____

*What year did you graduate
from YOUR HIGH SCHOOL?*
O 2009   O 2003
O 2008   O 2002
O 2007   O 2001
O 2006   O 2000
O 2005   O 1999
O 2004   O Did not graduate

*Approximately how long
were you enrolled at
YOUR HIGH SCHOOL?*
O Less Than 1 Year
O 1 Year
O 2 Years
O 3 Years
O 4 Years

*Which of the following best describes what you are currently
doing? (Select only one option)*
O Continuing my education and not employed
O Continuing my education and employed
O Employed part-time and not continuing my education
O Employed full-time and not continuing my education
O Self-employed (farm or business owner, etc.)
O Serving in the Armed Forces
O Caring for a home/family
O Unemployed
O Other _____

Indicate the highest level of education completed:
O High school not completed
O High school diploma
O High school equivalency test or GED
O Some college-level work completed
O Technical program certificate or diploma
O Associate Degree (two-year program)
O Bachelor's Degree
O Master's Degree
O Doctoral or professional degree
O Other _____

*How would you describe your individual
program of study during high school?*
O Business or commerical
O Vocational/occupational
O College Preparatory
O Advanced Placement
O General
O International Baccalaureate
O Other

*What was your overall grade
point average at the time you left
YOUR HIGH SCHOOL?*
O A+ (above 4.0)
O A– to A (3.5 to 4.0)
O B to A– (3.0 to 3.49)
O B– to B (2.5 to 2.99)
O C to C– (2.0 to 2.49)
O D to C– (1.0 to 1.49)
O Below D (0.0 to 0.99)

*How far from YOUR HIGH
SCHOOL are you currently
living?*
O Less than 25 miles
O 25 to 99 miles
O 100 to 199 miles
O 200 to 500 miles
O More than 500 miles

Section II: Continuing Education

Complete this section *only* if you ever attended a postsecondary institution (college, technical school, university, etc.), or are planning to attend such an institution during the next year. If you have *not* attended a postsecondary institution, and do *not* plan to continue your education within the next year, skip to Section III. *(Note: There is a place for comments at the end of this section.)*

For what reason did you decide to continue your education?
O To take a few job-related courses
O To take a few courses for self-improvement or personal satisfaction
O To take a course(s) necessary for transferring to another college
O To obtain or maintain certification
O To complete a vocational/technical program
O To obtain an Associate Degree (2-year)
O To obtain an Bachelors Degree (4-year)
O To obtain a Master's Degree
O To obtain a Doctorate or a professional degree
O To please my parents
O No definite objective in mind

*Approximately how many years of
postsecondary education have you completed?*
O I have not yet begun my postsecondary education
O Less than 1 year
O 1 to 1 1/2 years
O 2 to 2 1/2 years
O 3 to 3 1/2 years
O 4 to 4 1/2 years
O More than 5 years

Page 1 of 4 *(Continued)* ➡

Education for the Future

Alumni

Section II (Continued)

How well did **YOUR HIGH SCHOOL**
prepare you for continuing your education?

O Very well
O More than adequately
O Adequately
O Less than adequately
O Very poorly

> **Comments:**

Section III: Employment

Please respond to the following questions regarding your employment history since you left **YOUR HIGH SCHOOL**. Complete *only* the parts of this section that apply to you.

Part 1

Did **YOUR HIGH SCHOOL** *provide
assistance to you in choosing your career?*

O No, I did not ask for help from my high school
O No, but I needed help
O Yes, and it was helpful
O Yes, but it was not helpful

*Which of the following sources provided the most help in obtaining your
first full-time job after high school? (Select only one option)*

O High school counselors
O High school teachers
O High school administrators
O Parent or relative
O Newspaper/trade publication
O Friend
O Recruited by employer

O Public/private employment agency
O College placement office/counselors/faculty
O Part-time job during high school
O College professor
O College degree
O Choice of study
O Other _____

*Indicate how each one of the following affected obtaining your first full-time
job after high school:*

	No Influence	Minor Influence	Some Influence	Moderate Influence	Major Influence
Deciding what I wanted to do	①	②	③	④	⑤
Knowing how to find job openings	①	②	③	④	⑤
Scheduling interviews	①	②	③	④	⑤
Writing a resume, vita, or letter of introduction	①	②	③	④	⑤
Finding a job that paid enough	①	②	③	④	⑤
Completing a job application	①	②	③	④	⑤
Finding a job for which I was trained	①	②	③	④	⑤
Finding a job where I wanted to live	①	②	③	④	⑤
Finding the kind of job I wanted	①	②	③	④	⑤
Discrimination because of my age, race, gender, etc.	①	②	③	④	⑤

Page 2 of 4 *(Continued)* ━━━▶

Education for the Future

Alumni

Section III (Continued)
Part 2

*Which of the following **best** describes your current type of occupation? (Select only one option)*

O Clerical or secretarial worker (typist, bookkeeper, etc.)
O Craftsman or foreman (carpenter, bricklayer, etc.)
O Farmer, rancher
O Laborer (construction worker, longshoreman, etc.)
O Bench worker (assembler, welder, etc.)
O Professional (law, medicine, etc.)
O Technical (medical, technician, etc.)
O Education (teacher, administrator, etc.)
O Proprietor/manager, business owner
O Sales worker (retail sales, insurance sales, etc.)
O Heavy equipment or vehicle operator
O Service worker (janitor, cook, etc.)
O Hotel Management (Parks and recreation management)
O Other _____

How closely related is your current occupation to the occupation you planned in high school?

O Does not apply; I had no clear plans in high school
O Highly related
O Related
O Slightly related
O Not related

*How well did your education at **YOUR HIGH SCHOOL** prepare you for your present occupationn?*

O Very well
O More than adequately
O Adequately
O Less than adequately
O Very poorly

Indicate your satisfaction with each of the following aspects of your present job:

	Not Satisfied	Minimally Satisfied	Somewhat Satisfied	Satisfied	Highly Satisfied
Challenging	1	2	3	4	5
Location	1	2	3	4	5
Salary and benefits	1	2	3	4	5
Advancement potential	1	2	3	4	5
Working conditions	1	2	3	4	5
Career potential	1	2	3	4	5
Meaningfulness	1	2	3	4	5
Other	1	2	3	4	5

Part 3

Complete the questions *only* if you are currently unemployed. If not, skip to Section IV.

*Indicate the **primary** reason you are now unemployed:*

O Have been unable to find a full-time job
O Was laid-off by employer
O Quit to find another job
O Health/personal reasons
O Do not desire employment at this time (in school, traveling, etc.)
O Other _____

*How long have you been **actively** seeking employment?*

O Not seeking employment
O 1 to 3 months
O 4 to 6 months
O 7 to 11 months
O 1 to 2 years
O Over 2 years

Page 3 of 4 *(Continued)* ➡

Education for the Future

Section IV: Everyone Complete

YOUR HIGH SCHOOL has helped me feel ready for the out-of-school world, with reference to:

	Strongly Disagree	Disagree	Neutral	Agree	Strongly Agree
My ability to write	①	②	③	④	⑤
My ability to read	①	②	③	④	⑤
My ability with mathematics	①	②	③	④	⑤
My ability to process information	①	②	③	④	⑤
My ability to use technology in the workplace	①	②	③	④	⑤
My speaking skills	①	②	③	④	⑤
My ability to learn on my own	①	②	③	④	⑤

Knowing what you now know, what changes need to be made at YOUR HIGH SCHOOL?

Thank you!

Education for the Future

Organizational Learning

NOTE: This PDF file is for content review purposes only—*not* intended for use in questionnaire administration. For more information about administering and analyzing *Education for the Future* questionnaires, please visit: *http://eff.csuchico.edu/questionnaire_resources/*.

At the ORGANIZATIONAL LEVEL of learning:

Statement	Strongly Disagree	Disagree	Neutral	Agree	Strongly Agree
Our district has a shared vision.	①	②	③	④	⑤
We communicate the lessons learned from our past actions throughout the organization.	①	②	③	④	⑤
Our district's Strategic Plan has been clearly communicated to me.	①	②	③	④	⑤
Our district has measurable goals for student achievement.	①	②	③	④	⑤
Our district's Strategic Plan goals are used as criteria for decision making.	①	②	③	④	⑤
Information about the district's organizational performance has been clearly communicated to me.	①	②	③	④	⑤
In our district, data about performance are collected systematically.	①	②	③	④	⑤
Needs identified in employee performance reviews are used to plan professional development.	①	②	③	④	⑤
Needs identified in data analysis are used to plan professional development.	①	②	③	④	⑤
Our district retains talented employees.	①	②	③	④	⑤
The flow of new ideas throughout the district is encouraged.	①	②	③	④	⑤
Our district ensures effective communication across the organization.	①	②	③	④	⑤
Our district fosters collaborative decision making.	①	②	③	④	⑤
Our goals are supported by clearly defined procedures.	①	②	③	④	⑤
Schools/departments who meet goals share strategies across our organization.	①	②	③	④	⑤
Our district encourages constructive collective-bargaining arrangements.	①	②	③	④	⑤
When my bargaining unit/association experiences problems with the district, procedures are in place to resolve them quickly.	①	②	③	④	⑤
Our district's focus on continuous improvement is making a difference in student learning.	①	②	③	④	⑤
Our district's culture is characterized by a high degree of trust.	①	②	③	④	⑤
Our district has high, ethnical standards.	①	②	③	④	⑤

At the TEAM LEVEL of learning:

Statement	Strongly Disagree	Disagree	Neutral	Agree	Strongly Agree
My school/department is treated with respect.	①	②	③	④	⑤
Innovation is encouraged in my school/department.	①	②	③	④	⑤
My colleagues have opportunities to share knowledge.	①	②	③	④	⑤
Members of my school/department cooperate to achieve our objectives.	①	②	③	④	⑤
The needs of each member of a group are taken into account when making decisions.	①	②	③	④	⑤
Opportunities are provided for discussion of best practices among my colleagues.	①	②	③	④	⑤
My school/department is prepared to rethink decisions when presented with new information.	①	②	③	④	⑤
My school/department has access to the information we need to make informed decisions.	①	②	③	④	⑤
My school/department knows how to tell if we are making progress on our measures related to the district's Strategic Plan.	①	②	③	④	⑤
My supervisor effectively aligns our school's/department's work with district goals.	①	②	③	④	⑤

Page 1 of 3 *(Continued)* ➤

Education for the Future

Organizational Learning

	Strongly Disagree	Disagree	Neutral	Agree	Strongly Agree

At the TEAM LEVEL of learning *(Continued)*:

	Strongly Disagree	Disagree	Neutral	Agree	Strongly Agree
My school/department uses data to improve our work procedures.	①	②	③	④	⑤
Schools/departments have the tools to use data to improve performance.	①	②	③	④	⑤
The district provides professional development opportunities for my school/department to try out new practices.	①	②	③	④	⑤
My bargaining unit/association has opportunities to influence the district's direction.	①	②	③	④	⑤

At the INDIVIDUAL LEVEL of learning:

	Strongly Disagree	Disagree	Neutral	Agree	Strongly Agree
I enjoy my work.	①	②	③	④	⑤
I have a safe workplace.	①	②	③	④	⑤
I go above and beyond to get my job done.	①	②	③	④	⑤
I see a clear link between my work and the district's goals.	①	②	③	④	⑤
I understand how my work contributes to the performance of the district.	①	②	③	④	⑤
I know how to measure the quality of my work.	①	②	③	④	⑤
I am aware of the critical issues that affect my work.	①	②	③	④	⑤
I apply what I learn in training sessions to my daily activities.	①	②	③	④	⑤
My supervisor understands the challenges of my job.	①	②	③	④	⑤
My opinion is respected concerning changes that affect my work.	①	②	③	④	⑤
My accomplishments are recognized.	①	②	③	④	⑤
My contributions make a difference to my school/department.	①	②	③	④	⑤
There are measurable outcomes directly related to my job performance.	①	②	③	④	⑤
Results of district progress in achieving our goals lead me to review my own practices.	①	②	③	④	⑤
I am encouraged to continually update my skills.	①	②	③	④	⑤
Adequate resources are provided for me to get my job done effectively.	①	②	③	④	⑤
The use of technology has made me more effective in my job.	①	②	③	④	⑤

Page 2 of 3 *(Continued)* ▶

Education for the Future

Organizational Learning

What are the strengths of this school?

What needs to be improved?

Demographic Data

For each item, please select the description that applies to you. These demographic data are used for summary analyses; some descriptions will not be reported if groups are so small that individuals can be identified.

Ethnicity:
(Mark all that apply.)

- ○ American Indian / Alaskan Native
- ○ Asian
- ○ Black (African-American)
- ○ Filipino
- ○ Hispanic / Latino
- ○ Pacific Islander
- ○ White (Caucasian)
- ○ Other

Gender:

- ○ Male
- ○ Female

I am a(n):

- ○ Elementary Assistant Principal
- ○ Elementary Principal
- ○ Middle School Assistant Principal
- ○ Middle School Principal
- ○ High School Assistant Principal
- ○ High School Principal
- ○ Other School Administrator: _____
- ○ District Administrator
- ○ Specify: _____

I have been in my current position:

- ○ 1st Year
- ○ 2–3 Years
- ○ 4–6 Years
- ○ 7–10 Years
- ○ 11–14 Years
- ○ 15–20 Years
- ○ 21–25 Years
- ○ 26+ Years

I have been an administrator for:

- ○ 1st Year
- ○ 2–3 Years
- ○ 4–6 Years
- ○ 7–10 Years
- ○ 11–14 Years
- ○ 15–20 Years
- ○ 21–25 Years
- ○ 26+ Years

Thank you!

REFERENCES AND RESOURCES

Beaudoin, M.N., & Taylor, M. (2004). *Creating a positive school culture: How principals and teachers can solve problems together.* Thousand Oaks, CA: Corwin Press.

Bernhardt, V.L. (2009). *Data, data everywhere: Bringing all the data together for continuous school improvement.* Larchmont, NY: Eye on Education, Inc.

Bernhardt, V.L. (2007). *Translating data into information to improve teaching and learning.* Larchmont, NY: Eye on Education, Inc.

Bernhardt, V.L. (2005). *Using data to improve student learning in school districts.* Larchmont, NY: Eye on Education, Inc.

Bernhardt, V.L. (2004). *Using data to improve student learning in high schools.* Larchmont, NY: Eye on Education, Inc.

Bernhardt, V.L. (2004). *Using data to improve student learning in middle schools.* Larchmont, NY: Eye on Education, Inc.

Bernhardt, V.L. (2004). *Data analysis for continuous school improvement.* Second Edition. Larchmont, NY: Eye on Education, Inc.

Bernhardt, V.L. (2003). *Using data to improve student learning in elementary schools.* Larchmont, NY: Eye on Education, Inc.

Bernhardt, V.L. (2002). *The school portfolio toolkit: A planning, implementation, and evaluation guide for continuous school improvement.* Larchmont, NY: Eye on Education, Inc.

Cameron, K.S., & Quinn, R.E. (1999). *Diagnosing and changing organizational culture.* Reading, MA: Addison-Wesley Publishing Co., Inc.

Colton, D., & Covert, R.W. (2007). *Designing and constructing instruments for social research and evaluation.* San Francisco, CA: Jossey-Bass Publishers.

Cox, James (2007). *Finding the story behind the numbers: A tool-based guide for evaluating educational programs.* Thousand Oaks, CA: Corwin Press.

Cox, J.B., & Cox, K.B. (2008). *Your opinion please! How to build the best questionnaires in the field of education.* Second Edition. Thousand Oaks, CA: Corwin Press.

DeVellis, R.F. (2003). *Scale development: Theory and applications.* Second Edition. Applied Social Research Methods Series, Volume 26. Newbury Park, CA: Sage Publications, Inc.

Dillman, D.A., & Bowker, D.K. (2001). *The web questionnaire: Challenge to survey methodologists.* Working paper available from *http://survey.sesrc.wsu.edu/dillman/papers.htm*

Dillman, D.A., Tortora, R.D., & Bowker, D. (1998). *Principles for constructing web surveys.* Working paper available from *http://survey.sesrc.wsu.edu/dillman/papers.htm*

Dillman, D.A., Tortora, R.D., Conrad, J., & Bowker, D. (1998). Influence of plain vs. fancy design on response rates of Web surveys. Working paper available from *http://survey.sesrc.wsu.edu/dillman/papers.htm*

Fink, A., & Kosecoff, J. (1998). *How to conduct surveys: A step-by-step guide.* Second Edition. Thousand Oaks: CA: Sage Publications, Inc.

Glasser, W. (1998). *The quality school: Managing students without coercion.* Second Edition. New York, NY: HarperCollins Publishers, Inc.

Greenbaum, T.L. (1998). *The handbook for focus group research.* Second Edition. Thousand Oaks, CA: Sage Publications, Inc.

Kouzes, J.M., & Posner, B.Z. (2002). *The leadership challenge: How to keep getting extraordinary things done in organizations.* Second Edition. San Francisco, CA: Jossey-Bass Publishers.

Peterson, R.A. (2000). *Constructing effective questionnaires.* Thousand Oaks, CA: Sage Publications, Inc.

Ramsey, R.R. (2007). *Don't teach the canaries not to sing: Creating a school culture that boosts achievement.* Thousand Oaks, CA: Sage Publications, Inc.

Redline, C., & Dillman, D. (2002). *The influence of alternative visual designs on respondents' performance with branching instructions in self-administered questionnaires.* In R. Groves, D. Dillman, J. Eltinge, & R. Little (Eds.), Survey nonresponse. New York, NY: John Wiley & Sons, Inc.

Saris, W.E., & Gallhofer, I.N. (2007). *Design, evaluation, and analysis of questionnaires for survey research.* Hoboken, NJ: John Wiley & Sons, Inc.

Silverman, D. (2001). *Interpreting qualitative data: Methods for analyzing talk, text and interaction.* Thousand Oaks, CA: Sage Publications, Inc.

Thomas, S.J. (2004). *Using web and paper questionnaires for data-based decision making: From design to interpretation of the results.* Thousand Oaks, CA: Corwin Press.

INDEX

NOTES

NOTES